Bambi and Me

Bambi and Me

Michel Tremblay

translated by
Sheila Fischman

Talonbooks
1998

Published with the assistance of the Canada Council.

Talonbooks
#104—3100 Production Way
Burnaby, British Columbia, Canada V5A 4R4

Typeset in Adobe Caslon and printed and bound in Canada by
Hignell Printing Ltd.

First Printing: March 1998

Talonbooks are distributed in Canada by General Distribution
Services, 30 Lesmill Road, Toronto, Ontario, Canada M3B 2T6;
Tel.:(416) 445-3333; Fax:(416) 445-5967.

Talonbooks are distributed in the U.S.A. by General Distribution
Services Inc., 85 Rock River Drive, Suite 202, Buffalo, New York,
U.S.A. 14207-2170; Tel.:1-800-805-1083; Fax:1-800-481-6207.

Les Vues animées was first published in 1990 by Leméac Éditeur
Inc., Montréal, Québec.

Canadian Cataloguing in Publication Data

Tremblay, Michel, 1942-
[Vues animées. English]
Bambi and me

Translation of: Les vues animées.
ISBN 0-88922-380-7

1. Tremblay, Michel, 1942- 2. Authors, Canadian (French)
—Childhood and youth. 3. Motion pictures. I. Title.
PS8539.R47V8313 1998   C848'.54   C98-910283-1
PQ3919.2.T73V8313 1998

Contents

to my mother and my father
for whom motion pictures
were always les vues animées
and not yet simply les vues.

The literature of memory is the last refuge of the rabble.

Umberto Eco
Foucault's Pendulum

Had I known that one day I would have a story,
I would have chosen it, I would have lived it more carefully
so it would be beautiful and true, with a view to pleasing myself.

Marguerite Duras
La vie tranquille

Life is a tragedy for those who feel
and a comedy for those who think.

*(Found in a Chinese fortune cookie on the day I
finished this book, 24 July 1990, in New York.)*

Orphée

Death created an awful lot of smoke with her cigarettes. She'd take a drag, hold her breath for a long time, then disappear behind a whitish screen I thought was gorgeous. Somebody, an old geezer with a mustache I think, asked: "Do you love that man?" She took another drag on her cigarette, didn't answer. He asked again, more harshly: "Madame, do you love that man?" Death looked at Jean Marais. Right smack in the eyes. "Yes."

I nearly fainted. I'd actually seen Death come every night and with her big she-wolf's eyes that chilled my blood watch Jean Marais sleep, but I'd never in a million years have suspected that she loved him. She was Death, and Death cannot love; when she looks at a person with those she-wolf's eyes, she's going to kill him! Actually, Jean Marais looked as stunned as I was myself. I knew he loved Death, he'd just told François Périer he did, and I was exasperated because I thought his wife was nicer, more gracious, prettier, even if she didn't seem all that bright. But for her, for this character who looked like a ghost in a black dress, with her bikers who run over poets and that way she had of bringing people back from the dead by making them pass through mirrors after she'd put on dishwashing gloves, for her to have the nerve to come out with that demure little "Yes"—I was shocked.

My mother was blowing her nose. Whenever a woman told Jean Marais she loved him, my mother blew her nose.

She'd even sobbed outright when Edwige Feuillère dragged herself to his feet at the end of *The Two-Headed Eagle*. But Death! I mean, really!

I knew I was watching an actress, of course. I was old enough to understand that it was a movie, I was twelve years old, but this was the first time I'd seen Maria Casarès; I didn't like the look of her and I'd decided to play naïve. I pretended I believed what I was seeing and I hated, I absolutely despised this Death character who was going to do everything in her power, I knew it, to take Jean Marais away from his poor pregnant wife. I imagined what would come afterwards (I already had a tendency to guess how a movie was going to end): Jean Marais would follow Death into her devastated land where old women pushed empty baby-carriages and young men whirled through the street crying: "Glazier! Glazier!," Euridyce would stay there by herself, well, no, not altogether, because François Périer loved her; anyway, it would end badly like all French films, I would be frustrated because I hadn't really understood the message and once again, I was going to have a terrible time getting to sleep.

The geezer with the mustache was finding Death guilty of I can't remember what crime and I was glad. As for her, tough luck.

"You like those kinds of movies?"

It was Monsieur Migneault, our boarder, who'd just slipped into his seat at the dining-room table to watch a little TV with us, as he did all too often. His cheap perfume the whole family had been complaining about for months made me sick and I thought I was going to throw up. We looked at each other, my mother and I, disheartened. We'd managed to persuade my two brothers and my father to let us enjoy our French film in peace, and now Monsieur Migneault, who had trouble grasping the thread of *14, rue de Calais*, was forcing himself on us without even asking permission.

"Who's that? You ask me, it looks stupid. Hasn't she got any lips of her own? Is that why she had to paint them on?"

Even though I more or less shared his opinion, I heaved a big irritated sigh in the direction of my mother. Who took the situation in hand.

"Monsieur Migneault, this movie's been running more than an hour, so don't start asking us questions.... We aren't going to summarize what's happened so far, it's hard enough for us to understand it ourselves!"

"You mean you're watching something you don't understand?"

"Maybe we will at the end...."

"What if you don't, then what'll you do?"

"Don't worry, Monsieur Migneault, if we don't understand we'll feel silly, that's all, but you've made us miss an important part and now we'll understand even less!"

"They aren't even talking now!"

"I told you before, on television, even when they don't talk you still have to watch. And keep quiet.... Just because they aren't talking doesn't mean it doesn't mean anything."

"It's pretty damn boring...."

"Well, if that's what you think, you can always go back to your room."

He folded his hands, sheepish as a child who's been caught with his face in a cake that was being kept for company.

"Okay, I'll shut up."

I'd been hoping he'd leave. My mother looked at me helplessly. The smell in the dining room was getting stronger and she started fanning herself, ostentatiously. But it was impossible to make Monsieur Migneault understand something without drawing him a detailed picture.

We turned our attention back to the film. And now we really couldn't understand a thing.

François Périer and the poet who'd been the first one to get killed at the beginning of the film was strangling Jean Marais, no less, even though they'd been friends from the outset, while Death kept repeating: "Go on, get going! Harder! Harder! Work!" while she rolled her big white eyes. I was starting to think she was going too far. That they were all going too far.

"So does she like him or not!"

Monsieur Migneault coughed into his fist.

"If you ask me, none of it makes any sense."

My mother slapped the table, hard, with the flat of her hand.

"Go back to your room or go to the tavern with my husband, Monsieur Migneault, but get out! Now! You'll make us miss the end!"

He left the room, hunched over like an old man, muttering: "I still can't believe you actually like that!"

My mother rubbed the palm of her left hand.

"I'm sure I burst some veins there!"

It was the end. Pushed along by the two guys on bikes, Death and François Périer were moving away, disappearing into a source of light where floated a large quantity of smoke that reminded you of what Death produced with her cigarettes. The shot was very long, very slow. You saw them from behind, the guys on bikes holding on to their shoulders, Glück's music, which I was hearing for the first time, spellbound, swirled around them—the celestial flute, the sublime description of the Elysian Fields that would spend a long time at the top of my personal hit parade—enveloping them like the smoke. They were becoming very small, insignificant. Death was trivial now because of a love affair gone sour.

Then something happened that I couldn't understand. All of a sudden my heart rose into my throat, I felt as if I was going to fall on my face, I was bent double, shuddering: for the first time in my life I felt that ball of emotion, uncontrollable and often surprising because you aren't expecting it, that beginning now I would experience so often in the movies and at the theatre, that moment when all your resistance crumples and you surrender, total-ly helpless, to a work of art, to part of it, a single image or a well-delivered line, a movement that approaches great-ness or a lighting effect that's imprinted on your memory forever, that privileged moment, often so brief, for which the culture-glutton would give away part of his soul. I didn't know the name for what was happening inside me, but I already knew I'd do anything to make it happen again, it was at the same time so good and so upsetting, good enough that I didn't want it to end and upsetting because I was positive I could die of it. Death, once again.

I must have gone white, because my mother got out of her rocking chair, came over and touched my arm, her hand dry now from dozens of years of dishwashing and marked with blue veins that you wanted to kiss.

"Sometimes it doesn't matter if we don't understand, does it?"

Cinderella

Across the screen, the name Walt Disney unfurls in beribboned flourishes, pink on a blue background. All the minor characters gather around the heroine who is wearing, not her ball gown but the dress with the torn hem in which, every day, she's humiliated by her wicked stepmother and her even wickeder stepsisters. She's smiling though, as if she were posing for a family portrait. Because this *is* her family, the real one, the family of her heart, that's gathering around her: the two mice, Jack and Gus, wearing the little sweaters and the microscopic tuques she knit for them, her first present after she'd caught them in a trap, for their own good, so she could educate them, make them into her friends; the other mice, those who don't have names but are still very present in our heroine's life; the dog, a nice amiable-looking guy with his droopy ears and droopy smile (everything about him seems to be pulled towards the bottom, he's conical, a conical dog!); the little flock of birds, all of them blue, their wings spread wide even though they aren't flying, as if they're going to greet me with their song, their whistle actually, because in this movie the birds whistle. Only animals, for the good reason that humans are so cruel to her. Of course her fairy godmother is there, with her magic wand with the star sparkling at its tip, but is a fairy human, even if she assumes the shape of a cheerful, chubby little woman?

The music is about to start, I know the music's about to start. Which of the six or seven songs will we hear under the titles? "So This Is Love," which the heroine sings during the ball, in the arms of the Prince who's already swooning with love? Yes, probably. It's the sweetest, the most languorous, the one they have to put on right away under the titles so the audience will recognize it when it first appears or if, like me, they're seeing the movie for the fourth time in one day. But the music doesn't start. The image freezes, as if it's been blocked by a malevolent hand, the hand of someone who doesn't want the film to start or who doesn't want *me* to see it. Walt Disney's name stays up there, insistent and omnipresent, but the rest of it doesn't come.

A shudder. Every nerve in my body lets go at the same time. I feel as if I've missed the top step in a staircase. And then I open my eyes.

I'm lying on the living room sofa that serves as my bed. In the next room, one of my brothers is snoring. I saw *Cinderella* three times today, I'm still thrilled, bowled over, and just as I was falling asleep I'd ordered my brain to project it for me one last time. It didn't work.

I try humming "So This Is Love." Like that, yes, that's right, I've got it; yes, that's the tune, now I remember....

***

The day before, I'd wakened early. Right away, I remembered this was an important day, a day I'd been anticipating with a lot of excitement but with my mind in a fog, maybe because of my agitated sleep, and it took me a few minutes to remember why: today was Saturday, the first day of summer holidays and I was going to see Walt Disney's *Cinderella*. I'd come out with a loud "Yippee!"

when I got up and then a pillow landed on my head because it was only a quarter to seven.

***

I'd seen the ad in *La Presse* a week before, and according to my mother, the mention "a show for the whole family," gave me a case of St. Vitus Dance whenever it appeared in the paper. *Snow White, Pinocchio, Dumbo, Bambi* had all come out before I was born or when I was still too little to go to the movies and I'd only heard about them from my brothers and my cousins, but this time I was big enough to check the paper myself, I kept my eyes peeled for shows for the whole family and nobody could stop me from going to see *Cinderella*, even in English.

My mother asked:

"Where's it playing?"

I raced back to look in the paper.

"At the Outremont."

"That's the other end of the earth! I don't even know where it is!"

I'd pleaded with her, promised mountains of good behaviour, promised I'd be as good as gold all summer, promised years of running errands without grumbling, till finally, with a half-smile, she told me to go easy, one promise was plenty. And the one she picked was good behaviour for the whole summer. Which was going to be very hard as a matter of fact, since my whole gang—the Jodoins, the Beausoleils, the Rouleaus and the Guérins— were staying in town, and for a whole gang of kids between eight and ten to stay out of trouble all summer was practically impossible. So I'd arrange things so the others would get the blame, swearing to my mother afterwards that it wasn't my fault, they did it....

All excited, I'd raced over to tell Ginette and Louise Rouleau: Guess what, I'm so excited, there's a brand-new Walt Disney movie, *Cinderella*, it's in English but I'll understand anyway, it's at the Outremont and my mother's going to take me! And then in a great burst of generosity I told Madame Rouleau that my mother wanted to know if Ginette and Louise could come too. Amazingly, she said yes right away and I ran home to tell my mother that Madame Rouleau wanted to know if we could take Ginette and Louise to the movies with us.

Luckily, they didn't consult one another and my white lie went undetected.

My two brothers had laughed at me a little, claiming cartoons were for babies; but my cousin Hélène shut them up, saying they were the ones who always laughed the loudest during the cartoon at the Passe-Temps. To which my brother Bernard replied that *she* never laughed during the cartoon because she was too busy french-kissing just about anybody. My aunt Robertine, Hélène's mother, smacked my brother on the head, he started to howl, my mother joined in, a fight broke out between the two sisters-in-law and the possibility that I wouldn't get to see *Cinderella* hung over me all evening because it was on account of me, indirectly, that everything had happened.

That night, my mother had treated my father to one of her violent outbursts about how crowded we were that always ended with: When are we going to have our own apartment just for us, I can't take this any more, I know she's your sister but if this goes on I swear I'll murder somebody and you'll have to bring me oranges in jail for the rest of your life....

I made myself as small as possible; as usual, I waited till the wave had passed before I brought up *Cinderella* again.

***

"Three streetcars! You're going to take three streetcars to get to the movies! You're nuts!"

"I'm sure as heck not taking a taxi, they cost a fortune! And I promised the kids; I can't break my word just because it's far away."

"Isn't it showing anywhere else, in the west end maybe, the Loew's or the Capitol...."

"Of course not, it's only showing there. It'd be too simple if they showed it some place that was easy to get to!"

My mother had her hat on and she was already holding my hand tightly. We were out on the balcony with Aunt Robertine, waiting for my two friends to leave their house and come down to the sidewalk. Aunt Robertine was sipping her second Coke of the day. It was eleven a.m.

The day was infinitely sweet. Not too hot, the July humidity was still a long time away, it smelled of the St. Jean Baptiste holiday and stale coffee, and you wanted to throw your head back and drink in the air while you thought: Summer's here, the holidays have just started and *Cinderella*'s showing at the Outremont, this is happiness, this is what they mean by happiness and nothing else.

"You ever go to the Outremont, Bartine?"

"Are you kidding? I'm not even sure if it really exists!" One last slurp, one last belch poorly concealed behind a hand folded vaguely into a fist, then she plunked the empty bottle beside her chair.

Letting go of my hand, my mother started to pull on her crocheted white gloves, which as usual would leave red marks on my palm and the outer edge of my index finger. My hands would be numb and wrinkled for long minutes.... My mother always insisted on holding my hand when we went out; it was humiliating and it left marks besides!

"I'm in such a state! D'you think we have to go on tiptoe on the sidewalks in Outremont?"

She laughed nervously. My aunt gave her chair a good push and it started rocking a little too hard. The back of it banged into the brick. She swore.

"Apparently you have to talk bilingual in that part of town. Even more than downtown."

For both women Outremont was *terra incognita*, a forbidden country where the rich walked around all day greeting one another and asking if they've heard from their children who were studying in Europe to become lawyers like their fathers; for me, it was a new word that I liked the sound of, a beautiful, musical word that I savored as I said it over and over in my head. Hearing it, I divided it in two right away and I thought, hey, there's something on the other side of the mountain…. Every day I could see the mountain at the end of Mont-Royal Street, like a wall around my world, a natural conclusion to what I was allowed to know; but here I was learning something new: there was another neighbourhood, another city that was the continuation of Montreal beyond what I'd thought was the end of the world.

When I asked my mother what exactly does Outremont mean, she'd told me: "It's a place where people like us clean the houses." And the natural barrier had shot up again, by itself.

Ginette and Louise came out on their balcony, which was right next door to ours. My mother took my hand again and pulled me toward the stairs.

"Okay, let's get moving. We're in God's hands."

Aunt Robertine had crossed her arms the way she did whenever she shut herself off to any discussion, or when she wanted to hide her feelings.

"You got everything? Your purse, your money?"

She worried to see us setting out on such a long trip, but she was playing the part of the coolly rational woman concentrating on the practical details, leaving any pointless and cumbersome emotions aside.

My mother stopped right in the middle of the staircase. Her straw and sky-blue plastic purse hung from her arm.

"Don't scare me like that, Bartine, I haven't gone yet!"

Ginette and Louise were waiting at the foot of the stairs, as jumpy as fleas in their neatly ironed Sunday dresses crackling with starch. Their mother too was out on their balcony. She waved at us.

"Do you know where you're going at least, Madame Tremblay?"

My mother hesitated briefly. Should she tell the truth and risk seeing two little girls howl with grief because their mother had called them back home instead of letting them go out with a crazy neighbour, or take a deep breath and tell a white lie and hope her sister-in-law wouldn't open her big mouth....

I started the white lie and my mother was grateful, I could tell.

I gave them my most confident smile.

"My mother knows Montreal like the inside of her pocket!"

Madame Rouleau crossed her arms, a little like my aunt Robertine.

"That's just it, where you're going isn't Montreal!"

***

No problem on Mont-Royal Street. For my mother, the number seven streetcar was practically her second home; she knew all the conductors, some of them even by name, and she'd automatically take her place on the first straw seat and ask about their wives and children. They would answer her with a smile, always polite, and said good-bye very warmly when she got off, usually on St. Lawrence Boulevard where she regularly visited the dry goods stores, leaving behind her exhausted sales clerks and devastated stores, after she'd spent a huge fifty cents.

I was sitting between Ginette and Louise and we were talking about *Cinderella*. Ginette, at nine already the intellectual in our gang, wondered what version of the story Walt Disney had used: she'd read five or six and they all had different ending: either Cinderella punished her stepsisters or she made them her servants or else she forgave them—and sometimes the story didn't even say what happened to them....

I couldn't have cared less about how the movie ended; I was interested in the supporting characters you could see in the newspaper ads—the mice, the birds, the cat, the dog, the fairy—but not Cinderella or her Prince or her stepmother or her stepsisters.... The humans in animated cartoons were extremely boring; I liked the weirdness of the barely recognizable, fantastically caricatured animals, with their funny voices, their incredible adventures, their jerky movements and elastic bodies. Anything could happen to them—an iron slammed in the face, a ton of bricks landing on the head, a piano, an anvil—but you always knew that at the end of the next sequence, they'd be intact and ready to tackle the most bewildering situations with the same blind naiveté, while the humans were always desperately the same: a little stiff, not so realistic that we'd grow attached to them, but with all their limbs in the right places to respect proportions and plausibility. Totally boring. And the last thing I wanted an animated cartoon to be was plausible.

As for my friends, they were already dreaming about the Prince (they said Prince Charming, almost pronouncing the capital letters, as if that was his name): Ginette wanted him to be blond and friendly and probably cultivated; Louise wanted him to be dark but not absolutely black and most of all, handsome and gallant like a Hollywood movie star. And they had lively discussions about the colour of Cinderella's ball gown: white would be too much like a wedding dress, a colour wouldn't be chic enough, so what could it be? Not black, that's for sure! To put in my two cents' worth, I suggested green, my favourite colour, but they nudged each other and giggled and told me for maybe the two hundredth time that boys don't have any taste. So then I asked Louise how come she had a green ribbon in her hair and she told me a ribbon isn't a dress and besides, it wasn't green, it was green*ish*. It was green and I said so very loud and my mother had to step in before a fight broke out.

***

Just after St. Denis Street, my mother stuck her head outside.

"It's clouding over. Don't tell me it's going to rain, and me in just a housedress."

The conductor, Monsieur Gariépy, a man in his fifties whom she thought was very nice, leaned out to get a better look at the sky.

"Well, the forecast said there'd be storms."

"Don't tell me. I should've listened to the radio this morning.... Oh Lord, I just hope we get there before it starts...."

Needless to say it began to rain the minute we got off at the corner of Park Avenue, a wonderful heavy rain that wouldn't last long but would create havoc. Just as a street-car pulled up, going in the direction of Bernard Street, my mother waded into the traffic, desperately flailing her arms. Over the storm you could hear horns blaring and bells clanging and the four of us raced towards the street-car—which took off without waiting for us.

My mother let fly some words I'd never heard her say before and again started waving her arms, trying to stop a car, a taxi, anything that was heading north and would take us along. We were already soaking wet when a taxi deigned to stop—after copiously splashing us. My mother got in the front, the three of us in the back.

"What do you kids want to do? Go home and come back tomorrow when the weather's nicer?"

Cries, howls, protests.

"We can't go to the movies like this, we'll catch our death of cold!"

Protests, howls, cries. And my mother gives in, sighing and wiping her neck with her already soggy handkerchief.

Now for the first time she spoke to the taxi driver.

"Outremont Theatre, please, and make it snappy."

The driver hesitated a few seconds.

"Where's that?"

My mother froze in mid-gesture.

"You're the driver, not me.... Don't you know where the Outremont Theatre is?"

"I don't have to know buildings, lady, just streets!"

"How stupid can you get? Now ask me nicely and I'll tell you what street it's on!"

"What street is it you want, lady?"

"You still aren't very polite, but I'll tell you anyway. Bernard Street. At the corner of Chapdelaine or maybe it's Champagneur or Champagne—something like that."

"You're the one that's supposed to know.... So which is it? Champagneur or Champagne or Chapdelaine?"

"Look, just let us off at Bernard and Champagne or Champagneur or Chapdelaine, and that's where it'll be. Seems to me you ought to know your streets! Is there a corner of Bernard and Chapdelaine?"

"No."

"How about Bernard and Champagne?"

"Nope."

"Bernard and Champagneur then?"

"Yes."

"That's it then, dummy! Now quit wasting my time! Are you laughing at me or what? I'm soaking wet and I'm on my way to see some lousy cartoons, so don't you start bugging me now on top of everything!"

"If you don't like it, you know, you can always get out."

"No, I don't like it and I'm not getting out in the rain, that's for sure! Now get moving. You've got a green light and I can't wait to see *Cinderella*! I'm going to catch my death of cold watching the Mickey Mouses do their somersaults and make their funny faces but I want you to know, I'm excited!"

She pretended to cough and I slumped deeper into the mouse-grey plush that felt prickly against my shoulder blades. I'd rather have gone home than watch her play sick like she always did when she ran out of arguments. And what if she was going to cough all through the movie to make me or all three of us feel guilty?

Louise sneezed and I could hear her sister mutter to her to stop or Madame Tremblay will think you're sick and we'll have to go home.... And in fact my mother had turned in her direction with a glimmer of hope in her eyes.

"Have you caught a cold, you little trouble-maker?"

Ginette thought fast.

"Oh no, she just wants us to pay attention to her!"

∗∗∗

My mother took a crisp new five-dollar bill from her purse.

"One child, three adults please."

Then she slapped her forehead.

"What am I talking about? Sorry, we had so much trouble getting here.... Don't know what I was...."

The cashier leaned towards the window separating her from my mother.

"I don't speak French. One adult and three children?"

My mother looked her straight in the eyes.

"What do we look like? Three adults and a child? How stupid can you get?"

∗∗∗

An obviously wicked lady with huge green eyes and a cruel smile that paralyzed you in your seat called to Cinderella. The little girl went to a dark corner where you could just make out an impressive canopy bed, then the shadow of the casement window slipped over her. The scene was ominous, mysterious. There was something not very nice between these two women, you could sense it. Rivalry, or some kind of jealousy. The older woman's eyes were too intense and the way the younger one moved was too meek, too submissive.... If she'd been a little more aggressive, the girl could have flung herself at the face of the lady in the canopy bed and that would have been absolutely the right thing to do. We'd have loved it. But something stopped her, an excess of goodness maybe, which made her an easy victim, and she kept her head down.

We weren't even in our seats yet and already I was so caught up in the action, the drawing, the colours, the movement—so natural—of the wicked woman's arms as she petted a magnificent black-and-white cat, who I suspected was the one hateful character of all the animals around Cinderella because his eyes weren't honest and his smile was downright hypocritical. I couldn't understand what they were saying but I guessed that the wicked woman was giving nasty orders to the young girl. Cinderella, humiliated, hung her head and nodded; the cat looked delighted.

Unable to see two steps ahead of us in the darkened theatre, all four of us stood in the central aisle waiting for our eyes to get used to the dark. It already smelled of popcorn, a child was crying and my mother was muttering.

"Haven't they got any ushers? What kind of place is this anyway? Are we supposed to stand here for the whole show? If I have to dry out I'd just as soon do it sitting down!"

Someone nearby went "Ssssh!" so close to us it made my mother jump.

"Good Lord, I nearly sat on somebody and I didn't even know it!"

A tiny little woman came running up, holding a flashlight and apologizing in English. My mother pushed the three of us, a little too hard, if you want my opinion, because Louise nearly fell on her face in the aisle.

"Come on, hurry up before she decides she doesn't feel like showing us to our seats...."

We'd disturbed a whole family of Anglos, father, mother and kids, who stood up very reluctantly to let us by. My mother said: "Excuse me, excuse me" so loud, some more people in the theater went "Ssshhh!" Then, as soon as she was in her seat, she started fidgeting. She squirmed, she tugged at her dress, she fanned herself.

On the screen, Cinderella was singing as she washed the floor. Soap bubbles floated up into the room, her image was multiplied, twelve, fifty, a hundred Cinderellas were scrubbing the floor and humming "Sing Sweet Nightingale," all drawn alike but in different colours, some garish, some subtle, against a black background. Everything was round and soft, even the movements: bubbles drifted slowly past our eyes while Cinderella plunged her hands into a wooden bucket circled in iron, her image rounded in the convex surface of the soapy spheres. I was ecstatic. The music was wonderful, the images gorgeous, I was sitting between my mother and my two best friends and I could have watched that sequence for hours: the multiplying bubbles, Cinderella who seemed happy despite the lowliness of her task, the beauty of the music.... But then, suddenly, all the bubbles burst simultaneously: the big cat, whose name appropriately was Lucifer, had deliberately left paw-prints all over the floor and on the stairs, and Cinderella would have to start over again. He moved away, showing us his fat rear end, with a satisfied backward glance as if he was thumbing his nose at us all. Children's protests could be heard all over the theatre. As far as I was concerned, hating that cat was fun. I wished for him the worst tortures that could befall a cat. A bath maybe? Yes, Cinderella ought to give him a bath!

My mother leaned over to me.

"Look, this is ridiculous, my dress is sticking to me. I'll go to the washroom and try to dry off, they must have paper towels or something…. If I sit here in a wet dress till it dries, I'll come down with rheumatism and all my fingers will get twisted…. I want you kids to wait for me; don't move!"

As if we had any intention of moving! Not even an earthquake would budge us!

Again she walked past the Anglo family. The father whispered something, she talked back in the same tone of voice. And I thought to myself: Oh boy, there's going to be a fight when she comes back!

＊＊＊

What I remember of the next hour is a sensation of choking with happiness. I laughed, I cried, I was scared to death; I rose up against the injustice represented by the other three female characters and that goddamn cat Lucifer and I jumped for joy at the triumph of reason in the form of a glass slipper tiny enough for Cinderella's dainty foot. I danced in the palace gardens to the rhythm of "So This is Love"; I helped Gus transport through an endless maze of stairways the key that would open the door to Cinderella's bedroom where she'd been locked up by her stepmother who, having recognized her as the mysterious beauty from the night before, wouldn't let her come downstairs to try on the slipper; I punished Lucifer the cat for all the trouble he'd caused (taking on the dog's role, I pushed him out of the tower where Cinderella lived and I barked for joy as I watched him fall); along with the mice, I sewed the blue and pink ball gown that the horrible stepsisters would tear to shreds, claiming the cloth it was made of belonged to them; I shivered when they pulled off the string of green beads, even though they'd thrown those same beads into the garbage can earlier; I drew arabesques in the sky while singing "Bibbity Bobbety Boo" as the pumpkin was transformed into a magnificent grey carriage and Gus and Jack into comical footmen; I threw rice at the wedding of the hero and heroine, again accompanied by Jack and Gus, my two favourite characters; I was no longer myself, a dreamy nine-year-old with an imagination, I'd merged into what I was seeing, I moved through the film along with the mice, the birds, the dog, the fairy; I was the magic wand and the pumpkin, I was the Prince and Cinderella, I sounded midnight, I was the clock that sounded midnight, the glass slipper that refused the stepsisters' feet, I was Walt Disney's movie and I would never ever leave it.

I'm sure my mother came back at some point, maybe she had a row with our neighbours, she must have asked me if it was a good movie, but none of it registered. Nor did Ginette and Louise and I talk about it, bowled over as we were, enchanted, overjoyed or scared silly, depending on what sequence was going on before our eyes.

When the newlyweds drove off in their carriage in the middle of a kiss and "The End" appeared on the screen I was exhausted. To say that I wished it would go on, that it would never end, would be an understatement. I wanted nothing more to do with reality, not even the summer that was just beginning, the days at Parc Lafontaine or on St. Helen's Island that I'd been promised for months. I was an animated Technicolor drawing and that was what I wanted to be forever.

The lights came on again slowly and the Anglo families started making their way to the exit. My mother leaned across to me, I remember she was holding an empty popcorn container. "Do you want to go now or do you want to stay and see the beginning of the show?"

I didn't need to answer. She put her hand on my forehead. "Have you got a fever, for heaven's sake? This is ridiculous, getting yourself so worked up over a cartoon! We'll watch the beginning and then we'll go…. I don't want the both of us to take sick: me with double pneumonia and you crazy on account of a children's movie…."

***

We sat through the whole film again, twice. My mother dried off without getting sick and I spent an afternoon in total rapture.

***

A while ago I watched *Cinderella* again. I bought the video as soon as it came out. I was afraid I'd be disappointed, of course, afraid I wouldn't be awestruck as I'd been at nine, afraid it would be ugly, flabby, manipulative, moronic. It had been a good thirty years since I'd seen it, since the time when I'd become a confirmed anti-Disney and flatly and irrevocably condemned his entire output, even my beloved *Cinderella*….

To my amazement I remembered every sequence, every shot, every line—funny or emotional—it was all as fresh as if I'd screened the film the day before. I laughed in the same places and to my great relief, there was no trace now of my late-adolescent disgust, when I swore by Fritz

Freleng and Chuck Jones and gagged at the mere name of Walt Disney.

But still there was a big surprise in store. This time I was absolutely enchanted by the wicked Lucifer, the cat I'd hated so much as a child! What a brilliant character! The drawing was at once sophisticated and simple, the movements graceful and flowing, the evil smile and the depraved eyes a sheer delight. That cat laps cream like no other cat before him, and the insidious airs he puts on are close to high art, he carts around his obesity with perfect grace, he pisses everybody off with obvious pleasure—in short, I adore that cat and I sometimes play the video just to see my idol pretend he's being tortured by the unbearable dog I now find totally boring, ugly, a suck. I like it when Lucifer smiles at the camera after he's pulled some rotten stunt; it's pure provocation, sublime hamming, and a shiver of admiration for such perfect nastiness runs down my spine. His grin widens into a thin hypocritical line, his almond-shaped eyes take on a diabolical expression, and I'm happy.

Eat your hearts out, Jack and Gus, you may be cute and comical but Lucifer's come into my life.

Is it possible that society has made me a cynic? Could be. Did the people who created that cat realize they'd made a great character whose genius only adults could understand? If they did they were successful, because now I dream of starting a fan club for my new idol: "The friends of Lucifer!"

Bambi

Did you cry as much as I did at the death of Bambi's mother? Personally, I've never got over it.

Snow White
and the Seven Dwarfs

I went back to the Outremont theatre just once during my childhood. It was for the rerun of *Snow White and the Seven Dwarfs*, also by Walt Disney.

It was a movie I knew by heart even before I'd seen it: my two brothers, Jacques and Bernard, and my three cousins, Hélène, Jeanne and Lise, had told me the story dozens of times, they'd even mimed for me, sung me the main songs (Hélène stood at the dining-room window in profile to perform "Some Day My Prince Will Come" and I swooned) and they also used it to scare me whenever I bugged them on Saturday night, especially Lise who loved to console me when I was terrified.

I was the youngest in the family and they were all old enough to baby-sit me when our parents got together to play cards; they took turns, often grudgingly because everybody knows the most boring thing in the world is looking after a little brat on Saturday night, especially one that won't go to bed....

I loved it though because with each of the five I'd spend the evening in a very different way: my brother Jacques instilled the rudiments of classical music in me (he'd made up a story to Ponchielli's "Dance of the Hours" that's still intact whenever I happen to hear that excerpt from *La Gioconda*); Bernard threw parties with his friends, festivities that started early and finished late, always noisy with plenty to drink, that inevitably ended in closets or the bathroom; Hélène polished her nails tirelessly while confessing her love stories—mostly unhappy but always incredibly romantic—with streetcar drivers, nightclub waiters, or underlings in the small Montreal Mafia; Jeanne would tell me stories she'd made up, based on fairy tales we knew all too well (her version of "Little Red Riding Hood", murmured with all the lights out, was particularly terrifying) and brought me the latest family stories, often numerous and always juicy; while Lise would act out the scene with the poisoned apple from "Snow White," in costume and with amazing acting talent.

While the others brought out "Snow White" to get rid of me when I refused to turn in for the night, using every expedient the story suggested to track me through the house and guide me to my bed where, panicking, I'd finally take shelter, convinced the hunter was going to deliver my heart to the evil queen or that the animals in the forest were going to eat me alive, Lise made the movie the very heart of the evening, a kind of inevitable ceremony as exciting as it was scary, during which Snow White (me, draped in a sheet) was sacrificed to the servants of Evil personified by the witch with the big nose and the devastating laugh (her, disguised in an old chenille bathrobe of my mother's, hunched over, tiny, gesticulating, cackling, absolutely terrifying).

The ceremony always unfolded in the same way. Lise would turn off the radio where Tino Rossi or Luis Mariano was singing his heart out in praise of the beauties of Marinella or the women of Mexico, she'd knit her brow and say with a tremor in her voice, "I think I hear something on the gallery...." I'd act scared (I was, actually a little, but didn't want to show it), go to the dining room window, slowly push aside the grease-stained curtain and ask: "Do you think it's *her*?" When I turned around, Lise wasn't there in the dining room. I'd take off like a bullet, I'd hide in the bathroom whose door didn't lock, and wait. The evil queen. The witch. The murderess who was going to take it out on me because the mirror had told her she wasn't as fair as I was.

Shuffle. Glide. Shuffle. Glide. Someone, with calculated slowness, was limping across the kitchen. Her. I was so worked up I peed sitting on the toilet, like a girl. A voice …something like a cross between the cawing of a crow and a head cold that won't clear up, was saying: "Snow White? Snow White, is that you in the toilet?" Terror stopped behind the door, scratched. "Snow White? Are you in the toilet?" Silence. I wanted to answer but I couldn't. I was voiceless. Lifeless. A knot of fear. The door opened abruptly. A tiny silhouette, all hunched over, was holding a white sheet in front of herself. "Snow White? How would you like a juicy red apple?" I let myself be wrapped in the shroud, I played dead, the witch picked me up in her arms, crossed the kitchen again, deposited me on the dining room sofa, a boat from another age covered in red velvet that had witnessed the elation of my first reading; the sheet was cool, I felt limp, I was drifting. When I opened my eyes, a juicy red apple, a real one snitched from the fruit bowl that always sat in the middle of the dining-room table, a poisoned apple that would put me to sleep—me, Snow White—for hundreds of years, apple of death, apple of love also because one day my prince would come, a perfectly ordinary apple but one that contained all the danger in the world, was swaying over my nose.

I imagined the seven dwarfs singing "Hi Ho" in their diamond mine, unaware of the danger I was in; I could guess at the damp muzzle of the fawns, the squirrels, the rabbits pressed against the dining-room window; I bit into the apple, thinking about that little runt in the plumed hat who maybe, some day, would deign to bend over and kiss me (after a hundred years, yuck, my breath would stink to high heaven!); I abandoned myself to my cousin Lise's fantasies which so easily became my own. And I died. I was good at it because there was a moment of wavering, of doubt between us before Lise said: "Michel? Are you okay?" Then she resumed her role. Which now consisted of crying, howling, tearing her witch's clothes off her back, rolling on the floor, mad with remorse, insulting the mirror that still refused to tell her she was the fairest one of all even though I was dead. Then it was her turn to die, cursing me, in a great tragic scene that sometimes went on a little too long. Her twisted hand rose in the dark room, it trembled, a dying voice murmured: "Your husband won't be any better than the rest of them, you stupid idiot, he'll cheat on you with any floozy that looks at him twice!" She shivered, coughed, rolled on the floor; this was her big moment and she pulled out all the stops. Then silence, a little bump on the hardwood floor. The ceremony was over. The evil queen had paid with her life for the odious crime of my death. I was so exhausted I sometimes actually fell asleep in my shroud. When I woke up I was in my bed and my cousin Lise was drinking coffee and reading a magazine. "Another nightmare, eh kiddo?" And she'd come and console me. That went on for a long time and it felt good.

All this to say that "Snow White and the Seven Dwarfs" was a lot more than a story for me, it was an adventure I'd lived several times, that was part of my personal terrors and joys. So the movie had its work cut out for it!

***

"Not the Outremont again! You'll never get there. It was hard enough for four of us to find last year, how do you expect to do it on your own?"

My mother of course still had an unpleasant memory of the Outremont theatre. Even if, and this I knew perfectly well, even if she'd loved the movie, she enjoyed telling anyone who would listen that she'd spent one whole afternoon in a soaking wet dress while she watched some rats sewing a ball gown.

But now I was old enough to take the streetcar by myself and I absolutely wanted to prove to the whole household that I could also go to the movies without a chaperone. There was a long debate on the question. My father was of the opinion that they should let me try my luck, while my mother, excessively protective, dramatic about everything, always worried about what could happen to her three sons even though the two oldest were nearly twenty years old, my mother said it was still too soon, movie theatres were full of maniacs, the Outremont was at the other end of the world, it's one thing to take one streetcar on your own but when you have to take three you can easily get lost and if anything happened to me they'd both be responsible and never, ever, would she forgive herself for losing a son just because she'd let him go to see a cartoon by himself. At the end of her exposition I was dead and buried, and my mother dressed in mourning for the rest of her days. But from the half-smile I thought I saw on my father's face, I knew I had a chance. He had let her talk, blow her nose, glimpse the horror of the little white coffin and the cemetery in the rain, but then he had burst out laughing, putting his arms around her and forcing her to waltz with him.

"You've got such an imagination, Nana—Jean Després should hire you to write *Jeunesse dorée* when she gets tired! You just described a whole season! I've always thought you should have been an actress. Marthe Thierry would've paled in comparison."

She laughed and I knew I'd won.

My mother had a sense of the dramatic, my father, of the ridiculous. Which made them a perfect match. My mother, intelligent as she was, often constructed incredible tragedies that my father took a perverse pleasure in tearing down with just one of those pithy remarks that were his specialty. They laughed, they tried out a few dance steps in the dining room and my mother said: "You win again, you old clown! One of these days you'll drive me to drink!" This time, though, she added, half-serious: "I'm not sure you're right.... Ten years old.... When I was that age I was still tied to my mother's apron strings...." To which he replied, "So's he, more's the pity."

***

The ad in *La Presse* said the first show was at half-past eleven. I left the house at half-past ten, proud as Punch, my money safe and sound inside a knot in one corner of my handkerchief (two quarters for the movie, two nickels for the streetcar, a dime for a Coke and another quarter just in case). I ran into my friend Jean-Paul Jodoin; I'd already told him I was going to the show by myself, but he didn't believe me. I offered to pay his streetcar fare so he could come and watch me walk into the Outremont.

"Are you kidding? How d'you expect me to get home by myself?"

"Just do the same thing backwards, dummy."

"My mother won't let me...."

He took a few steps away.

"I still don't believe you."

Wounded, I took my handkerchief from my pocket, undid the knot and held aloft the coins.

"And what do you think this is?"

He counted the money.

"It's ninety-five cents! I don't think I ever saw that much money at the same time."

"Now d'you believe me?"

He hesitated, scowled.

"I believe you've got the money but that doesn't mean you're going to the show. Maybe you're just doing some errand for your mother."

I could have killed him. Nothing in the world insults me as much as somebody doubting my word.

"I'm going to see *Snow White and the Seven Dwarfs*, in English, so there Jean-Paul Jodoin! It's at the Outremont theatre at the other end of the world and I know how to get there by myself even though you have to transfer three times! And when I come home this afternoon and tell you the whole story, then you'll have to believe me!"

He shrugged.

"So what. You're always full of baloney!"

✱✱✱

The journey was long, but simple: take the number seven Mont-Royal streetcar to Park Avenue, from there any car heading north to Bernard, then the only streetcar that goes along Bernard to Champagneur. I'd written it all out on a piece of paper along with my name, address and phone number, but I was a little ashamed of it and there was no way I'd take it out of my pocket, not even if I got lost.

It was a Saturday in May, slightly chilly, cloudy, and in my excitement before I left the house I'd forgotten my sweater on the living room sofa. My mother would make a fuss for sure but I tried not to think about it too much. She had a phobia about double pneumonia and bronchitis and right up till the beginning of June, she practically buried us under mounds of sweaters, scarves, tuques and caps whenever the sun disappeared. And I'm hardly exaggerating.

When I arrived at the Outremont, the doors were still locked. It was twenty after eleven, so I had ten more minutes to wait. I walked around the building, surprised there was such a fine theatre in a residential neighborhood (for us, movies theatres were always on busy streets where you could see them, not at the end of a rich, lifeless one where there wasn't even a restaurant), admiring the trees on Bernard Street, the houses on Champagneur, the well-tended lawns, which my mother and my two friends and I hadn't been able to do the year before because of the storm. I had a hard time understanding that just one family lived in each of these houses (we were three families squeezed into a seven-room apartment because we could eat more cheaply that way) and I tried to imagine climbing *up* stairs to go to bed in my room.... I couldn't do it. In spite of my powerful imagination. Tulips were freezing on a lawn and I thought about the only flowers that grew on my street in the spring: dandelions. I headed back to the theatre. Still no sign of life. Then I noticed a little card on one of the doors. The schedule. Which needless to say was quite different from the one in *La Presse*.

The first show was at one o'clock. It was half-past eleven, I was in a strange neighborhood, it was cold and there was no question of going home crying like a baby! So I had an hour and a half to kill. For a child of ten, an hour and a half away from home is like a whole day. An hour and a half to freeze, to not know what to do with my body, to pace up and down.... Tulips are pretty enough, but when you've seen one bed, you've seen them all! I cursed the newspaper, the theatre, Walt Disney who made movies that weren't shown at the right time, and I started pacing the sidewalk like an animal in a cage.

Once the initial panic had passed, I decided to walk to Park Avenue and look for a restaurant. I'd drink my Coke before the movie instead of during, that's all. But right near the theatre, set back a little, at the end of a short lane, I spied something—a bouquet of trees, a bridge, some paved paths—that looked like a park. In fact it was a park, but a tiny one, the smallest I'd ever seen, looking bedraggled in the harsh sunless light but beautiful anyway, because it seemed to have been designed for dolls, with a pond surrounding an island, a real little island where you could take refuge if you were shipwrecked, like me. And so I took refuge on the island where, to stave off boredom and pass the time, I imagined I might meet some extraordinary creatures, monsters out of the stories that haunted my sleep or fairies who would emerge from my books in three dimensions, whose images as they unfold jump up to your face when you turn the pages.... To dream for an hour and a half on a real island right here in Montreal, which was itself an island, wouldn't that be something!

It was too cold, the benches weren't set up yet and the lawn was wet. And you could travel around the island in just thirty seconds. Besides, a damp little wind had just come up and I was starting to shiver....

The only place that was sheltered from the wind was a little cement strip under the bridge, in the dark. I spent a good hour there railing, raging, crying (there were no witnesses), thinking I was the unluckiest child in the world, sure I was going to freeze to death and my stiffened body wouldn't be found for days, like the little match girl, that I'd be given a state funeral because I was a martyr of

La Presse, and Princess Elizabeth, my mother's favourite, the one who would become queen on the death of her father, the unmemorable George VI, would send my parents a telegram of condolence, along with a cheque for a million dollars like they'd done for the Dionne quintuplets, but it would be no use to me because I'd be dead.... My mother's influence, her nearly pathological propensity for the darkest tragedy, made me spend an hour that wasn't much fun, because I really was genuinely desperate, but in the end was fairly short and above all very intense. In the end I'd even forgotten I was going to the movies and had to run so I wouldn't be late.

Once again, the movie had its work cut out for it!

"If it's no good I'll kill everybody!"

But it couldn't not be good.

***

It was one of the bitterest disappointments of my life.

I didn't experience again last year's elation over Cinderella. And not for want of trying! But it all seemed bland, watered down, cutesy; I wanted to beat up Bashful who went around looking as if butter wouldn't melt in his mouth, Happy didn't make me laugh, he made me think of my uncles during family parties when they drank too much and went cross-eyed, Sneezy was disgusting because I hate it when people sneeze in front of me, I mixed up the other dwarfs whose "characteristics" I couldn't keep straight, the "yodeling" aspect of the film with its phony Alpine folk music got on my nerves, Snow White had less personality than her own Prince Charming, the animals in the forest weren't as much fun as the ones in the other movie, and worst of all, the wicked witch couldn't come up to my cousin Lise's ankles!

All because this time, I had an undeniable point of comparison: my own intimate knowledge of the story and a powerful experience that haunted my nights. A version of this movie had transformed my life as a child. All of which kept me from genuinely appreciating what I was seeing, my brain always functioning in a double perspective, between what I already knew and what I was looking at now, emphasizing the power of what I knew about the movie and which came from a vision that terrified me, and the film's intrinsic weakness, which was that it had been made for children. The movie had been produced to please; the story had been told to scare me. And I was annoyed at my cousin. After all, nobody had the right to be more terrifying than a movie, nobody had the right to be more talented than a movie!

I didn't shudder when the queen drank her magic potion and was transformed before my eyes into an insipid rubber Halloween mask. The children around me shrieked in horror and I felt like telling them, you ought to see our place on Saturday night when my cousin turns into a witch…. I'd never actually seen that myself but it was a lot worse than this because it happened inside my head! I wasn't scared either when the rubber mask held out the apple to Snow White, for the good reason that what the witch had to say wasn't nearly as terrible as hearing "Snow White? Are you in the toilet?" from my personal Pythia…. I didn't applaud when the dwarfs managed to hurl the witch into a ravine during a storm that came along very conveniently and made the stones slippery. And I thought the glass coffin was totally ridiculous. Besides, it must have reeked inside when the Prince opened it up! Actually, I retained one strong memory from the film, but I was still too numb from spending an hour waiting in the cold to be upset by it and try to figure out why I felt so flustered: Prince Charming was very handsome when he sang "One

Song," in an early sequence, while soppy Snow White just stood on her balcony and blushed.

The movie ended to thunderous applause. I was amazed. It was the first time in my life that one had let me down.

Needless to say I didn't watch *Snow White and the Seven Dwarfs* a second time, not even to check if I'd been right. I left the theatre with my head down, my hands in my pockets; it was still just as cold, I had an hour's streetcar trip ahead of me…. And I hoped that nobody in my family would ever tell me the story of a movie again!

La Fille des Marais

"That child's going to drive me crazy one of these days!"

My mother was tying her apron as she paced the kitchen. The beef and vegetable stew had finished simmering, now it was ready to serve. An absolutely intoxicating aroma had been drifting through the house for hours. The combined scents of carrots, celery, turnips, beef and herbs stopped you in your tracks and kept you from doing what you were supposed to be doing, even though it was Saturday and the weather was superb. Shadows had come several times to prowl around the stove, friendly but firm taps had been handed out when some particularly rash person had lifted the lid of the cast iron pot: "Don't touch, it mustn't lose its juice!" The household was at the table, the bread had been sliced and buttered, heads had turned in her direction, the goddess of the beef and vegetable stew who, instead of presiding over the much anticipated ceremony of dishing up the heavenly concoction, was raging against me because I hadn't come back from the movies.

"It's a quarter to seven and he's been gone since eleven this morning! I know he likes movies, but did he go and see six in a row?"

Now my aunt Robertine had donned her apron and moved to the stove.

"Want me to serve for you? Everybody's getting hungry...."

"My child could have been murdered in the La Scala theatre, watching Maria Goretti being carved into pieces, and all you can think about is eating!"

"He'll be here.... You know perfectly well, it takes him forever to get home from the show...."

"This is longer than ages! He could've let me know while he was at it, I'd've packed his pajamas and a lunch for tomorrow morning."

My brothers and my father hid their laughter in their plates, while my cousin Hélène simply shrugged.

"I'm going to the show tonight too, Auntie. At eight o'clock. And I'd really like time to eat without racing and get myself ready before I go! I've got better things to do than hang around waiting for that little snot-nosed brat.... Everything in this house always turns around him. You practically have to ask his permission to take a pee!"

Her mother jumped.

"Hélène, don't say dirty words in this house!"

"What dirty words? Did I say something dirty? Did I say shit? Did I say fuck?"

My father's sister stuck her nose in the pot.

"I knew it! I knew she'd say a real one! If she doesn't watch out I'll nick her neck with my potato peeler!"

My brother Bernard put on a mock serious look.

"Seems to me, Hélène, you aren't going to see Maria Goretti tonight...."

Hélène gave him a look as if she'd just noticed something sickening, a cockroach or a dead mouse.

"Who cares about Maria Goretti? I'm going to see Rita Hayworth! She's more my style. And a lot less stupid."

Her mother blew up, she couldn't stop herself.

"Hélène! The story of a saint isn't stupid! If you went to see a few more shows like that, it might put knock some sense into you."

Her daughter shrugged in a very elegant, very Hollywood gesture, head high, hair rippling and falling exactly where she wanted.

Slowly my father got to his feet and leaned in the kitchen doorway.

"Your beef stew's going to stick to the pot, Nana. Is there anything you hate more than food getting stuck to the pot?"

My mother stood facing him. She was very short and had to raise her chin very high to look him in the eyes.

"Yes! My child getting lost! Didn't I say he's too young to go the show by himself? It started with *Snow White* last month, now he won't let anybody go with him! He has a fit if I say I'd like somebody else to go along, he says we don't trust him and he'd look silly having an adult take him to the show."

"Nana, he went with about ten of his friends! When they left this morning it looked as if all the kids on Fabre Street wanted to move in with the Italians on Papineau Street!"

Taking advantage of this exchange between my parents, my aunt Robertine had lifted the lid of the stew-pot. She stirred the contents, inhaling the aroma. My brothers and cousins slipped into the kitchen, salivating.

My mother pounced on the wall-phone in the corridor that went to the front door.

"You're right! I'll call Madame Jodoin…. Maybe he's eating toast and peanut butter at their place…. Go ahead, the rest of you, eat it before it gets cold."

I'd written the Jodoins' number on the wall above the phone, which needless to say had got me a clout on the head at the time…. But my mother hadn't wiped it off. Just in case…. She found it instantly.

"That child writes so badly, I can't make head or tail of it. The teachers nowadays don't show them how to make their numbers. Besides messing up the wall you can't read it. Okay, I'll try an eight…. Maybe it's a three, but I'll try eight first…."

No one was listening to her now. The kitchen was abuzz with: "Give me some more, Auntie…." "No spuds, Ma, I'm on a diet…" "More gravy, just a little…. That's what I like the best, the gravy…." They practically ran to sit down and throw themselves at their plates.

"Hello? Hello, Madame Jodoin? Jean-Paul's mother? This is Madame Tremblay. Michel's mother…. Fine thanks, you? Actually, no, no I'm not fine at all…. Tell me, by any chance is Michel at your place?"

A beat. They can hear a voice but can't make out what it's saying. Everyone around the big table is eating in silence. They're relishing their meal but they've started listening again.

"I haven't seen him all day! How about your children, are they all there?"

Very brief silence, then the explosion.

"What do you mean, they've been back since three this afternoon! And Michel wasn't with them?"

The forks stayed in midair, my father was even starting to show the vertical wrinkle between his eyes that never heralded anything good. His rages were rare, but terrible.

"And why'd they leave him there? Why didn't they drag him with them by force!"

The voice at the other end rose a notch, my mother moved the receiver away from her ear.

"You don't have to yell! I know your kids aren't guardian angels, the way they smell!"

She hung up and leaned against the wall, her hand to her heart.

"He's dead! I told you, he's died a virgin and martyr watching Maria Goretti die a virgin and martyr! Say, how come they call her 'The Marais Girl' when her name's Goretti?"

My father went to her. You could tell from the slumped shoulders, from the slight trembling in his arm that my mother's anxiety was spreading to him too, he who was so self-possessed, so reflective. Even his voice was less assured than usual:

"If he's not home in five minutes I'll go look for him. I'll Maria Goretti him all right...."

My mother hung up the phone.

"Five minutes is too long, I'm calling the police.... If a child died in a movie theatre they'll know.... Dear God, what if he's already lying in a drawer in the morgue!"

My mother's hysteria (she'd practically yelled) seemed to bring her back to her senses and my father was nearly smiling.

"Now quit turning everything into a tragedy.... You almost had me believing you.... Why not just phone the theatre, that's a lot simpler...."

"You know, you're right. If they've just found him they must be wondering why nobody's called to claim him...."

"Want me to look up the number in the paper?"

"No, don't bother, the Bell girl will be quicker."

He came back to his place at the table, gesturing to everybody not to worry.

My mother dialed the operator, after misdialing twice. She cursed the telephone that wasn't working, bashing it recklessly. Finally someone answered.

"Hello, Mademoiselle, can I have the number of the La Scala movie theatre, my son's disappeared.... No, I don't want the number for the police, you nitwit, I asked you for the number of the La Scala theatre, on Papineau Street, because that's where he disappeared.... What do you mean, how do you write it? You write it the way you say it, in Italian! Oh no, don't start asking me to spell it, I'm upset enough as it is! You're the operator, not me! Aren't you supposed to know how to write things when the Bell gives you a job?"

She said nothing for a few seconds, her mouth agape, scandalized by what she was hearing.

"I'm usually perfectly polite, young lady, but right now I'm upset! I just told you, my child.... What? Well if you aren't allowed to chat on the phone, how come you're asking me all these questions, will you tell me that? Fine, give me your supervisor, I'll tell her a thing or two.... If you hadn't been wasting so much time since we started talking I'd've found him long ago! All right, so she's finally decided something.... Say that again, I didn't get that, you speak so badly...."

She slammed the phone down, nearly pulling it off the wall.

"I should've got her name.... Wasting my time like that.... Where do they get their employees anyway? From the lunatic asylum?"

She sat down on what we called the telephone chair, a decrepit old velvet armchair where all the women in the house would spend hours at a time, a warm Coke sitting on the floor, the newspaper or a magazine on their laps, the phone held tight against their ears.

My father looked up from his plate.

"You want me to call? You're too upset, you don't know what you're saying.... The poor girl.... It was you that was keeping her from doing her job...."

"I'm going to finish what I started! I'm going to drain the ciborium to the last drop!"

"Not the ciborium, Nana, the chalice...."

"What?"

"It's not the ciborium you drink to the last drop, it's the chalice...."

"Look, just leave me alone. I'll drink from whatever I want to drink out of. If my child's dead I want to be the first to know.... And I want to be the first to go and strangle whoever did it! They won't have to hang him, believe you me, I'll save them the trouble! And it isn't his neck he'll be hung by!"

My aunt Robertine had gone back to the kitchen. She served up second helpings of the beef and vegetable stew to whoever wanted any, which was everybody.

"Quit saying that all the time, Nana, you know perfectly well he's just late...."

My mother dialed the number of the theatre.

"He's never late for beef and vegetable stew! Never!"

Her sister-in-law came back to the dining room, her own plate nearly overflowing with succulent things that were making her mouth water.

"He didn't know we were eating beef and vegetable stew, we decided after he'd gone, for a surprise!"

My mother, who rarely paid attention when my aunt was talking, was already yelling into the receiver.

"Hello, Mademoiselle? Are you Italian? Can you speak French? Look, I'm not calling to ask when you're showing the show, I want to get my son back who disappeared from home at eleven this morning.... What? I'm talking too fast? You, an Italian, you're telling me I'm talking too fast? Can't you hear yourself? I couldn't understand you when you answered and I didn't ask you to repeat it! Now listen, is there anyone who runs things in that theatre, a boss, a manager, anything? Monsieur Minetti? Can I talk to him, can I talk to this Monsieur Minetti, please? Okay, give me his number, I'll phone him. Of course I'm going to disturb him! If it was your child that disappeared this morning in a theatre where children disappear, don't you think you'd disturb him yourself, your Monsieur Minetti? Okay, all right, pass him on directly, that'll save us all some time."

She put her hand over the mouthpiece.

"They're trying to tell me I've got no right to bother him! That's what a theatre manager's for, if you ask me, to be bothered. And he probably hasn't got a private number either.... Hello, Monsieur Minetti? I'm

Madame Tremblay, from Fabre Street.... Listen, my ten-year-old son.... Ah! so she's already told you.... It's true she talks fast, eh? Did you look and see if he's there? I know there's a lot of people but couldn't you just walk up the aisle and whisper his name? Not too loud, so you wouldn't disturb the others, but loud enough so he could hear you? His name's Michel.... If he hears you, he'll answer.... And tell him to get his tail home, right now! What's that? When's the next intermission? I can't wait that long, I'd go out of my mind.... And you could show a little politeness too! Listen, you've got a projector in your theatre.... Why not project his name on the screen.... Write something like: MICHEL TREMBLAY, YOUR MOTHER SAYS COME HOME FOR SUPPER. No, Monsieur, I'm not crazy, I've just lost my son and believe it or not, I want to find him! You're in a theatre, you're there to project things, so why can't you project that? Hello? Hello? He hung up on me! He's the one that killed him, I just know it! They make us think they're showing the lives of saints and then they kidnap our children!"

The front door opens suddenly, a stampede down the hallway and here I am in the dining room, red-faced and all out of breath.

"Does it ever smell good in here! What's for supper?"

My mother is glued to the spot, her hand on her heart, maybe even a little disappointed, unconsciously of course, to see me show up safe and sound before the end of one of the finest performances of her career.

My father wipes his mouth, puts down his napkin, gets to his feet and approaches me, hitching up his pants.

"We trusted you.... We let you go to the show like you wanted...."

He doesn't complete his sentence.

The slap is violent; my left cheek starts to swell up right away, even before I feel the pain.

"It's beef and vegetable stew. And I don't think I have to tell you, you're not getting any!"

It was the only time in my life my father slapped me; though what I needed wasn't a slap, it was an explanation. Because I hadn't understood what had happened to Maria Goretti.

✷✷✷

My father had guessed right, there were exactly eleven of us: Jean-Paul, Jean-Pierre and Marcelle Jodoin, Ginette and Louise Rouleau, Nicole and Roger Beausoleil, the Guérin twins, Gisèle and Micheline, their sister Pierrette and me. We'd gone to the La Scala theatre, at the corner of Papineau and Beaubien, on the number 45 streetcar, all excited because we rarely went to the city's north end, most of the forays by our respective families outside the Plateau Mont-Royal being made to what we called the bottom of the city, otherwise known as St. Catherine Street. For my friends and me, Montreal north of Laurier was a *terra incognita* that belonged to foreigners—not Anglos, others, Italians, except maybe Rosemont where some of us had relatives and where we'd heard they only spoke French.

I didn't have any relatives in Rosemont, I'd never even ventured into that part of town and I was looking eagerly out the window of the streetcar, expecting everything to change after the viaduct, that obvious barrier between the Italians and us, put up intentionally to keep us from socializing—as if we'd want to!

Actually, the only reason I wasn't afraid was that there were eleven of us. I don't know if I'd have gone by myself to this Montreal neighborhood, the Italian gangs, like our own Popeyes, having a very bad reputation and I myself being an avowed mamma's boy.

When we emerged from the viaduct I was a little disappointed because everything looked the same: three-storey houses with outside staircases and balconies with wrought-iron railings, exactly like the house where I lived, sidewalks crowded with children who looked like us, the perfectly French street names: Saint-Grégoire, Rosemont, Bellechasse, Beaubien…. But the name of the movie theatre was La Scala (my father had told me that meant "ladder" and right away I'd imagined a hall with very steep rows of seats where I was sure to get dizzy) and the cashier had the right accent: we were in a real Italian theatre, we were going to see our first Italian movie and we were as worked-up as a colony of ants who've spotted a sugar-cube.

A doubt took hold of Marcelle Jodoin though, just before we went inside:

"What're they going to talk, French or Italian?"

My mouth was already plastered against the first drinking fountain I saw (my mother said that I drank so much water I could beat the camels in the desert); I straightened up, wiping my mouth.

"If they didn't talk French they wouldn't advertise in *La Presse.*"

"Are you sure?"

My heart sank. I wasn't, not really.

"No…."

Eleven children pushed and shoved their way into the theatre. The screening hadn't started yet but we were reassured to hear the rest of the audience speaking French.

To our delight the film had been translated into our language and for what was probably the first time in my life, I heard the nasal voice of Nadine Alari which I would learn to loathe in years to come from hearing it too often: she dubbed the voices of all my American idols and a fair number of Italian actresses too.

We sat there very quietly during the screening. I think it was my first European film and it was all so different from what I was used to, my attention kept being drawn to details that had nothing to do with the story itself: (What a weird house! Why are the walls white plaster like that? How can they get along without running water? Do the animals really live downstairs from the people? That furniture looks really uncomfortable. I sure couldn't do that, take a boat to school every morning! Why are all the women dressed alike, why are the men so serious, why do they always keep their hats on?) that I had trouble following the action.

I had another problem too, one that also resulted from prejudices inherited from conversations I'd heard at home: I thought Ines Orsini was very beautiful as the pure Maria Goretti, but very blonde for an Italian. Italian women, so I'd heard, were anything but blonde.

I was still moved though when Maria Goretti discovered the ocean (lucky her!), I was troubled without actually knowing why when she pulled her skirt up above her knees before she walked into the water (though my eyes didn't bug out like her cousin Alexandro's did), I cried along with all my friends when she was stabbed by that same Alexandro, I even yelled, "Rotten pig!" with the girls, and at the end of the film I was relieved to learn that poor Maria had been named a saint because she hadn't yielded....

But yielded what? And to whom? I knew to whom because her cousin stabbed her forty-one times with his knife while she cried out no, no, no.... But what? What could she have that was precious enough to infuriate him like that?

At the end of the movie, the girls were dabbing at their eyes, the boys were clearing their throats, a little but not too much so they wouldn't look like sissies and I had an urge to lean across to Ginette and ask her the question that was nagging at me. But fear of being caught out not understanding a movie kept me back. Ginette and I read the same books, we discussed as equals the movies we'd seen in the parish hall, we had similar tastes and the same aversions, so I couldn't come out and admit to her point blank that I hadn't understood a thing about what we'd just seen!

Anyway, right after the film there was always a rush to the washrooms (the girls wondering if the seats were clean enough to sit on, the boys fully intending to piss on the seats because for once their mothers weren't there to yell at them) and I quickly found myself all alone next to the drinking fountain.

After buying the traditional Coke and the inevitable bag of Maple Leaf chips, we went on to the vote: we'd all liked it (except for Pierrette Guérin, the youngest, who was disappointed because she'd been expecting an animated film), and we all agreed to watch it again. Jean-Paul Jodoin even said: "That's the first time I saw the ocean too. Wasn't it beautiful!" And Nicole Beausoleil added: "Sure, but I bet it's even better in colour!"

During the second showing, less puzzled this time by the details of the Italians' daily life, I could follow the story better and I paid more attention to what was going on between Maria and her cousin.... I felt the same turmoil when she pulled up her skirt to go in the water, I thought Alexandro was just as weird when he rolled his big round eyes as he watched her swoon in the sea, I was

59

just as scared when he went up to her, gasping, at the end of the movie, and as she was backing up she bumped into the saucepans hanging side by side on the white wall (in fact those saucepans clinking together against a white background are one of those images that made the strongest impression on my life as a movie-goer), but I still didn't understand what was driving him so crazy. I mean, I had a kind of idea but it was so confused and so absurd, I was even more disconcerted than before: Maria was holding her skirt tightly against her while she shouted, "No," so whatever it was he was lusting after was there between her legs! Bits of conversation I'd heard at home, the incomprehensible jokes my brother Bernard told that made the women blush (though it didn't stop them from having a good laugh) came back to me and I was bothered even more.

So there was a game of life and death I didn't know yet, one that was played between men and women, a game of power in which the man held a knife and the woman refused.... And when the woman refused.... That was how I understood it because that was how it was presented to me. My first contact with sexuality, through the movies, was monstrous. But I didn't know it was about sexuality. I didn't even know sexuality existed. I was more than bothered, I think what I felt resembled anguish. Anguish at not understanding, but also fear of finding the answer to my questions, of finding there matters even more incomprehensible, even more mysterious, even more terrifying.

At the second intermission, my friends got up at the same time; no one was crying now, we'd seen the film twice (when I think of it, we actually said it dragged a little), it was a beautiful day outside, the park must be open, supper was over ages ago...and in any case, Pierrette Guérin had peed her pants.

They called me every name in the book of course when I told them I intended to stay; even Ginette couldn't understand why.

"Look, it wasn't all that good...."

Instead of confiding in her, trying to make her understand that I had a problem with the very core of the movie, with the essence of what it was that joined Maria to her cousin Alexandro, I barked:

"Well I liked it anyway, haven't I got the right to?"

Unaccustomed to hearing me sound so aggressive, she looked surprised.

"Sure, but it's two o'clock and we've been inside since eleven this morning...."

"I don't care, I want to see it again! And I'm not leaving till I know it by heart!"

She gave me a mocking little smile and I knew I wouldn't like what was coming next.

"Hey everybody, Michel's got a crush on Maria Goretti!"

They left the theatre screaming with laughter, in a wild stampede that brought protests from the audience. Just before going out, Jean-Paul Jodoin turned around.

"Next time he jumps on her, you'll try and save her, you jerk. Maybe you can change the ending so you can marry your beautiful Maria Goretti yourself!"

I was relieved to be alone. I'd be able to concentrate fully on the film, to study every sequence, every shot and try to find some indication—a movement, a word, a glance—anything that would help me understand. I didn't want to leave the theatre till I'd found a solution to the mystery of Alexandro's bulging eyes and the skirt Maria Goretti had pulled up and held on to at the same time.

A feeling of helplessness swept over me from the very beginning of the third showing: the film had given me everything it had to give me; nowhere was there a new key that could solve the riddle, the images filed past in the same way, the dialogue would explain nothing more, the film was frozen in space and time, definitively; and there I was looking at a wall that couldn't be scaled. I'd never be able to find out on my own. I needed someone to explain it. Especially, someone to explain why it was Alexandro and not Maria who was drawing more and more of my attention. It was his problem, his frustration I was interested in. I knew Maria was condemned but I wanted to know why, and it was through Alexandro that the solution would be found, I was sure of that. So I concentrated on him, so poorly described in the film, so inhuman, nearly a animal who was refused what he thought was his due. I listened to every word he said, I studied every one of his gestures, I tried to become him so I could read inside his head or at least feel his…his desire? I knew you could call it desire. But for what? I wished I could stand up and yell: "Please, somebody, tell me what he wants, it's driving me crazy!" Once again, the film ended and I didn't understand a thing.

And I'm fairly sure I cried with rage and frustration throughout the fourth showing. I was incapable of leaving the theatre, I'd achieved a degree of weakness that was close to unconsciousness, I was hypnotized by the screen where at regular intervals the same mysterious and irreversible images filed past, that I now knew by heart but that seemed to me less and less clear. I could recite the dialogue along with the characters, I could guess the shots before they appeared on screen, but I was no longer responding with either my emotions or my intelligence.

Faced with a problem in math I'd sometimes plug away, out of pure stubbornness and certainly out of pride too, till I found the solution and could go on to say, slightly conceited, that it was easy, you just had to think. But here, looking at the screen in the La Scala movie theatre, I thought for hours, perfectly aware that my helplessness would remain total, that the solution to my problem was beyond my grasp, and I could have died of shame.

At the fourth death of Maria Goretti, I felt a kind of nausea, something that resembled the disgust I sometimes felt at night when I'd just finished my dessert and my mother brought my brother Bernard the enormous steak that was his reward for a hard day's work. I'd had an overabundance of movies and I was very close to vomiting.

I found myself on Papineau Street without thinking about it, without even wanting it, feeling stunned and nauseated. I didn't have a watch but I knew it was late and that my worries were far from over. In the first rays of the setting sun, Papineau Street had taken on an amber tint, a few neon signs were already on, the Italians who resembled us so much had even started to settle in on their balconies, like us, to catch whatever cool air happened to come their way.

A streetcar arrived, going in the right direction. I plunged my hand into my pocket. I had one dime left. A child's ticket cost five cents. And then something absolutely amazing happened. Whether from genuine shyness or just fatigue I'll never know, but it seemed to me absolutely impossible, beyond my strength, beyond my grasp to ask the conductor for change, though I usually wasn't so timid. I had a dime, I needed a nickel, and I hadn't the faintest idea what to do. I knew I'd be incapable of holding out my dime to the conductor, of speaking to him, of explaining, of expressing myself, of....

It didn't even occur to me that I could just drop the dime in the box like a bigshot!

So I ran. Like a madman. From Papineau and Beaubien all the way to Fabre and Gilford. Non-stop. At least I don't remember stopping. Two, three streetcars drove past me. I was a little scared under the viaduct and my nausea came back because of the smell of dried pee. What I remember most of all is the pain that ripped through my chest when I got to the bottom of our staircase. And the absolute certainty that I was about to spend one of the worst nights of my life. And that I didn't deserve it.

Before going inside, I pressed my ear to the mail slot near the bottom of the door. My mother was on the phone. Taking very loud. About me. The police! She was probably talking to the police! They mustn't know. My consternation. My frustration. My lack of intelligence. Because I was a numskull, I knew that now.

Delicious smells came wafting through the mail slot. I was so hungry! But how could I sneak up to the table as if nothing had happened? The whole thing had to be minimized…. I decided to use flattery and spontaneity.

And all I got out of it was a fat cheek, an empty stomach (despite the tasteless Campbell's chicken soup my mother brought me in great secrecy around nine o'clock) and a night spent in anguish, knowing I'd wake up next morning even more thick-headed than I already was….

I didn't solve the mystery of Maria Goretti for quite a while and later on, at school, when I heard the joke about her for the first time: "The one that said no because she didn't understand the question," I felt it was aimed at me personally.

The Parade of the Wooden Soldiers

I was a little ashamed of the first real sexual fantasy I had at the movies. A few years ago I took another look at the character in question, in the film in question, and I had a shock: how could I have gone into ecstasies over somebody so nondescript, so totally lacking in sex appeal and—not to mince words—so ugly? Was it because, in the end, the emotion you feel from the very first sequence, the torment when you discover you've chosen the wrong person, the terrible and wonderful sense of abandon when you follow your heart and not your reason (or, rather, other people's reason) depended no more on that particular period in my life than on the very object of my desire? Wouldn't anyone else have served just as well simply because, at that point in my existence, when I was on the verge of adolescence, I was ready for passion?

I can laugh at it now because it all happened more than thirty-five years ago, but for a long time I was haunted by that summer afternoon when I discovered that I really wasn't like other people, that I had to accept it, and most of all, to live it. In 1955, that took nerve!

At the time we'd been living for a few years on Cartier Street, at 4505, just at the corner of Mont-Royal, over a drugstore that still exists but now has a Vietnamese name. My aunt Robertine had taken an apartment with her son

Claude, Hélène was married, my father's two brothers who for so long had "roomed" on Fabre Street had rented something near by, so we had an entire apartment to ourselves: my father and mother occupied the middle room, which was vast and bright, my two brothers and I had the double room that looked out onto Mont-Royal Street and the corner balcony, and Monsieur Migneault, whom I've mentioned before and who helped us pay the rent, had inherited my aunt's old room immediately to the right of the front door.

My mother was very happy; she had more privacy, her two older sons, her pride and joy, had jobs that paid very well, my father, despite his growing deafness, was still working, the baby of the family who'd arrived so late but whom she'd wanted so badly, was showing promise. She knew that I was writing. She didn't know what and she never asked to read anything, but I'm fairly sure she was glad there was someone in the family with a literary bent (to the degree that you can take seriously the dream of a child who had a strong tendency towards exaltation, but I think it was true in her case).

I was more and more in love with the movies, even more than literature, almost. I devoured everything on television, I was still going to "shows for the whole family" at the four corners of Montreal: from the Regent at the corner of Park and Laurier, to the Westmount in the neighborhood of the same name, to the Snowdon which I always had trouble finding, to the theatres on St. Catherine Street that I thought were so beautiful, so impressive, to Saturday matinées at the Saint-Stanislas parish hall, I'd now added the Friday evening shows in the church of St. Dominic, the English Catholic parish on De Lorimier Avenue. My English was good because I saw so many American movies and it was easy for me to imitate the French accent because of a talent for mimicry I subsequently lost. My mother and I were crazy about Jean

Marais, Georges Guétary (that's right!), Edwige Feuillère, Blanchette Brunoy, Jean Tissier, Annabella, Fernandel and Milly Mathis—my favourite actually, because she resembled my mother a little. I could fake the Marseillais accent of Orane Demazis in *Marius* to ask my father for money to go to the movies and the Parisian accent of Renée Saint-Cyr to tell my mother I didn't want any potatoes.

That Saturday, they were advertising a movie with Laurel and Hardy (whom we all called Aurel and Hardy, for reasons I never knew), *The Parade of the Wooden Soldiers*, a very loose adaptation of *Babes in Toyland*, an operetta by Sigmund Romberg adapted for the two great comics. Need I add that I was crazy about Laurel and Hardy, about their sense of the absurd and above all about big fat Hardy's bumbling manner when he fiddled with his necktie after he'd done something goofy? I nearly died laughing as I watched them lug a piano up a staircase during the entire half-hour film; I howled with delight when they tried to repair a boat motor in their last film, *Atoll K*, with Suzy Delair; I'd helped them set off the bomb in *The Big Boom*, which I'd seen at the Saint-Stanislas parish hall surrounded by the indescribable frenzy of delighted children; after that I was thrilled to see them in a movie based a Mother Goose tale. A movie with songs, no less!

I'd seen very few musical comedies but I was already very fond of the kind of absurdity that took over the screen when the characters, often ordinary people, started to sing and dance in mid-conversation as they went about their business. Later on, I'd develop a true passion for movies like *The Pajama Game* or *Damn Yankees* in which the workers in a pajama factory in the first film, baseball players in the second, would throw themselves into an elaborate production number at the drop of a hat, transforming a picnic into a motley ballet bursting with energy and a baseball diamond into a place where—and this was absolutely amazing—just before an important game, men in uniform would start dancing together!

The Champlain cinema had just been completely renovated and I couldn't believe my eyes: now we had a movie theatre in the east end that was just as beautiful and even more modern than the Palace, the Loew's or the Capitol, the pride of the west end where the projection, so it said in the paper, was the most perfect in the world. I was convinced that the projection at the Champlain would be even more perfect and that the Anglos—how naïve I was, how innocent!—would come all the way to the corner of St. Catherine and Papineau to see....

The carpet, which was thick and soft, had a design of interlaced palm and acanthus leaves in shades of red, gold and grey, and I was almost afraid to walk on it, holding on very carefully to my bag of chips and my Coke while I looked for a seat. Everything smelled new because the walls, which were covered with gold-coloured hangings, and the gorgeous carpet hadn't yet had time to be permeated with the pervasive and slightly sickening smell of hot popcorn drenched with melted butter. In fact, it didn't smell of the movies at all and I was a little bewildered.

Filmed, unfortunately, in black and white (I was already seriously infected with the Technicolor virus), the beginning wasn't too bad: the old woman who lived in a shoe with a flock of noisy children couldn't pay her rent so the landlord, the wicked Mr. Barnaby, all swirling cape, hypocritical little mustache and top hat—in a word, the dirty dog in all his splendor—demanded quite simply to be paid in kind (they didn't put it that way, this wasn't a Joan Crawford melodrama, but that's how you were supposed to interpret it)—if his tenant's daughter, the little blonde curly-head dressed like a shepherdess, would agree to be his wife, it would be his pleasure to erase the mother's debt. Otherwise: cash. Tomorrow morning.

Like all the children present and a fair number of the adults too, I was scandalized. I couldn't, though, express my feelings by yelling and flinging popcorn and chips at the screen like the others because I was alone and I was afraid I'd look weird if I started waving my arms around all by myself in my corner. And so I suppressed my anger and frustration by washing down a little too quickly my now soggy chips with a big gulp of cold Coke.

Luckily, Stanley and Oliver—whom we'd stopped waiting for, the action on screen was so gripping—came to the rescue and drove the evil Mr. Barnaby away in an absolutely hilarious scene where they played golf with spinning tops as balls, aiming them at the old woman's landlord. He fled like a rat after handing out the usual threats. The battle was won but not the war, because Mr. Barnaby was sure to come back and claim his due, as he'd put it so well. All the characters were very depressed.

Then something totally unexpected happened, something that was going to change my life. The young curly-haired blonde shepherdess—you'll have guessed that she was Little Bo-Peep—had, on top of everything else, lost her sheep and she was utterly forlorn (things were going very badly for her: she was in danger of ending up in the bed of a mustachioed old skinflint and she was out of a job). And so she retreated to the edge of a stream that flowed through a ravine to cry her little heart out and Tom-Tom, the local dandy and in a way her boyfriend, came and consoled her.

As soon as I saw him coming down the path to join his sweetheart I felt vaguely uncomfortable. I told myself it was probably because his costume looked something like Peter Pan's, to whom I'd devoted a tremendous passion since my early childhood: a leotard you knew was green, ballet dancer's tights and the plumed hat tipped coquettishly to the side of his head. But I wasn't sure. Something about him was attracting me but I wasn't quite sure what. His smile, maybe, which was gorgeous; certainly his frailty, because you could sense that he too had barely emerged from childhood and that questions of love weren't simple for him.

With a mustache, he'd have been Robin Hood and I would probably be saved for a while yet; without a mustache, he was Peter Pan and I was condemned to a truth that I hadn't been looking for, not at all.

I'd stopped listening to what either one was saying, I'd lost the thread of the story, I thought of hundreds of reasons to look at him, with no comprehension of the turmoil racing through me, that light-headed sensation when he smiled as he got a little too close to her, the conviction that at the very moment of his arrival I had just lost, and gained, something mysterious, precious, terrible. He sat down next to her beside the stream and he consoled her; we saw the two of them in close-up, confused and shy; we knew what they wanted, we wanted it too, but it was making them wait. Finally, they decided.

Were they singing? Probably. It was an operetta, after all. But I didn't even notice, already absorbed, hypnotized, overcome as I was by the revelation I was about to have. Because I knew that if they kissed, my life would change for ever. They looked at one another, slowly their heads came closer, their lips touched, just barely, but enough so you could call it a kiss...and for the first time in my life I was fully aware that I wanted to be in her place!

Recollections stuffed away in a corner of my memories and never explored came back to me then and I knew this moment wasn't really a revelation, it had been coming for a very long time, patiently waiting to come forward until the little boy I still was, was on the point of being transformed into a grownup.

***

When my brothers or my girl cousins couldn't or wouldn't baby-sit me on Saturday night during my early childhood, my parents had no choice but to drag me along with them. They played cards either at my aunt Marguerite's, my father's sister, my aunt Jeanne's, a distant cousin also on his side, or at my grandmother Maria's, my mother's mother, already very old at the time, a colourful character, a French-speaking Cree from Saskatchewan and proud of it, foul-mouthed for the sheer pleasure of being provocative, funny, a practical joker, though her frantic turbulence was a little scary. When she saw me arrive, she'd invariably come out with: "Look who's here, my daughter's latest sin!" then give me a noisy kiss, rumple my hair and forget me for the rest of the evening. Even though I didn't know what it meant, I hated being my mother's latest sin.

She flirted shamelessly with my father, saying she'd always found him to her liking. She exclaimed to whoever would listen that her daughter was a lucky woman and there were nights when she herself would gladly be content with some leftovers. Everybody laughed, good old Maria, isn't she crazy, except my mother who said, blushing, "Come on Mama, not in front of everybody!" To which her mother replied: "When you can't do something because you're too old, little girl, you laugh at it, for relief!" She'd give my father a loud smack, pretend to faint away in his arms, then cry out: "Let's get moving, you buggers, take out your money so I can clean you out!"

Playing cards was actually serious business and they got down to it quickly, with a kind of passion that was wonderful to see. They settled in around the old wooden table very early and got up from it very late, slightly haggard, overwrought from winning or losing four dollars and twenty-five cents, crumpled, happy. All evening long I'd heard them shout: "The littlest one's in the hole!"; "The pisser!"; "Three times lucky!"; "Baseball"—enigmatic and comical formulas that reminded me more of a primary school recreation room than a get-together of grownups. It was two or three a.m. and I'd been asleep for hours, either in an armchair or buried under all the coats on my grandmother's bed that winter and summer always smelled of camphor. My parents would wake me up, I'd whimper, my mother would say: "He was looking at a magazine when he fell asleep! I wonder what he sees in them...!"

Actually, I wasn't looking at the magazines, I was hunting for the Ipana toothpaste ads and I'd spend hours trying to penetrate their secrets. That was the memory that came back to me as I watched Little Bo-Peep and Tom-Tom kissing so ingenuously.

Those ads were nearly always the same: a man and a woman with a mouthful of healthy teeth looking at each other, smiling and about to kiss. They were never very young but they were always very good-looking. But that image of imminent pleasure concealed a secret that was meant for me, as I realized very early. I could sit there for ages, glued to my seat while I looked at those ads, I could melt into them, hypnotize myself from peering at them, I could *become* them, never understanding why, then I'd fall asleep, exhausted and invariably frustrated from missing the solution once again.

***

Now that solution had stared me in the face right there in the Champlain theatre, in the middle of a black-and-white operetta, looking at a totally nondescript actor wearing too much makeup, whose mouth was painted with what looked like black lipstick, and it upset me, a lot.

So that was it…all this time I just had to make a simple transference, imagine myself in the woman's place, and I'd have the key to the mystery! Because I didn't want to *be* the woman, I only wanted to be in her place, in the arms of Tom-Tom or the guy with all the teeth.

I don't know if I can say I was surprised; what I felt was not so much amazement as something close to fatalism: I knew it was going to happen, I'd always known, I didn't want to know, I hid it from myself to avoid facing up to it…. But now there it was, official, and I had to face up to it!

I need hardly add that I've got only a very vague memory of the rest of the film: I remember that Laurel and Hardy were dunked in a pond after being tied to a kind of seesaw, that at the end of the movie wooden soldiers, hundreds of them I think, came and rescued everybody, that Barnaby was punished, the old woman who lived in a shoe got her revenge, the lovers were reunited, Laurel and Hardy were happy. And the other children in the theatre were thrilled. But all that was vague, like a dream you can remember only bits of, and so ordinary next to what I'd just discovered!

I was stunned when I left the theatre. But for once it was for reasons that had nothing to do with the movie I'd just seen.

***

I walked back up Papineau Street. Even the heavenly aroma of Weston's bakery couldn't shake me out of my torpor. I climbed up the Sherbooke hill without realizing it and found myself in Parc Lafontaine. They'd just put out the benches which had been repainted a brilliant green since last fall, signs reading "Ne passez pas sur le gazon— Do not trespass!" had sprung up like mushrooms, there was a smell of freshly-cut grass. I sat down across the street from the Notre Dame hospital where I was born and as always, I looked for the window of the room my mother had been in, at any rate the one she'd shown me once when we were taking a walk, telling me it was the one. I was quick to believe her of course. It was just over the main door, a little to the right, a window easy to recognize, that I could still find automatically without even looking whenever I walked past the hospital.

I leaned my head against the back of the bench and I wondered very seriously what had gone wrong that day, in that hospital room, to make me what I was. I mean, I didn't know yet exactly what I was. But I knew I'd wished I were in Little Bo-Peep's place and in the place of those ladies in the Ipana toothpaste ads when they kissed their boyfriends, but what that really meant about me I didn't know. And the rest, how you experience it, how you *do* it, and where and with whom, I had no idea about either, and I had a hunch that finding out was going to be hard if not impossible.

Because in the end the thing itself, perhaps because of my vast ignorance of sexual realities, was still less terrifying than its direct and immediate repercussions on my life. I couldn't forget, I couldn't act as if I didn't know, I certainly couldn't talk about it to my friends or to anyone in my family, so it was something I had to keep to myself, maybe forever, like a lump in my throat, yet it was something essential, an important secret I'd want to share but had to stifle inside me, repress at all costs so I wouldn't be repudiated, driven away, cursed. Because I knew that if the word ever got out, I'd be cursed, by everyone—and probably quite rightly! How, unless you're crazy, can you dream about being in the arms of a man who's just brushed his teeth with Ipana?

Was there anyone else like me on Fabre Street, a friend, a classmate with whom I could share this weighty secret? How could I find out? How could I talk about it? And how.... I pictured Jean-Paul Jodoin and Roger Beausoleil, my Fabre Street friends I still hung out with, who were starting to seriously eye the girls.... What was I going to talk with them about? About Tom-Tom, about his ballet dancer's tights and his feathered hat? And my new friend Réal Bastien whom I liked so much and who went around with a photo of Lucille Ball that he showed to everybody, saying there's nothing in the world as gorgeous as a red-head....

And what did it all mean? What was it exactly? A disease I'd come down with at birth, a corruption produced by society, a taste that develops unbeknownst to you because of...because of a...because of what? I knew the word to describe all that, several words even, each one uglier and more grotesque than the other, expressions that were used to express mockery, disgust, contempt. But that was all. Words.

I was facing a wall. I had no answer to the thousands of questions assailing me. I wanted to die. Seriously. Just outside the room where I was born. To die so I could erase all that. So I wouldn't have to understand it or, even worse, to live it.

I bent over double. I cried. For a long time. Snot poured from my nose, I wiped it off with my arm, I pressed my hands over my eyes to stop the tears, I knew my face was puffy and smeared, my mother would grill me when I got home.... For the first time I felt as if I was all alone in the world, an expression I would often repeat later on, when I began to write in order to relieve myself, to confess, to purge myself of a secret that was too great for me, one that even later on, I'd put into the mouths of characters in my plays to express helplessness.

Helpless to understand not just what was happening to me but who I was and how I'd ever manage to live the rest of my life, feeling tired and depressed, I went home, allowing myself all the same to dream about Tom-Tom, about his smile, about his fragility which surely must resemble my own.... Not much relief in the circumstances, but relief all the same. I was sitting by the stream.... I'd lost my sheep.... I was crying...and behind me I could hear the sound of footsteps....

Coeur de Maman

During my childhood there were very few Québécois films (we still called them French-Canadian) and I was still too young to go to them.

I vaguely remember hearing my mother and my aunt Robertine talking about *Tit-Coq*. What had most struck my aunt in that film was the presence of the cat during the supper scene at the beginning, and the final scene at the station that looked like "the real end of a real French movie." And they agreed that "our actors are just as good as the ones from France, and they haven't got a Gratien Gélinas in France!" I also remember hearing them talk about *L'esprit du mal*, in which Denyse Saint-Pierre, the oh so beautiful, oh so sweet Denyse Saint-Pierre, played an evil woman who I think was suffering from a venereal disease, but I'm not sure, maybe I'm confusing that film with the famous play by Paul Gury with the subtle title *The Deadly Kiss*, immortalized by Roger Garceau in which, to suggest the havoc wreaked by syphilis, he was decked out in a Halloween mask that terrified the spectators and maybe turned them off sex for good.

My family, at least the younger members—my brothers and my girl cousins, and the men—my father and his two brothers, Fernand and Gérard—were more drawn to American movies than to French ones, if I remember correctly; in any event, I heard more talk about Susan Hayward and Tyrone Power than about Michèle Morgan and Henri Vidal. At least till the arrival of television, when my mother and my aunt absolutely threw themselves on anything that was called a French film, serious or not, tragic or melodramatic, musical or not, to stave off their boredom as women whose children were growing up and who saw with dread the imminent end of their reign. American films had been their dream; French films were their refuge.

As far as the "French-Canadian" films were concerned, it took an event like *Tit-Coq* to persuade my family to bestir themselves, my mother and my aunt anyway. They hadn't gone to see *Un homme et son péché* or *Séraphin* because listening to the radio programme based on those two novels about the miser Séraphin was enough for them (and anyway my mother said that Hector Charland's voice always made her want to clear her throat); they'd missed *Le rossignol et les cloches* because Nicole Germain got on my mother's nerves: she thought she was snobbish and cold; nothing in the world would have made them spend money to see *Le grand Bill:* my aunt Robertine didn't like laughing in the movies, she said she went to the show to cry and if she didn't cry, she'd wasted her money.

My first Québécois film then was *Coeur de maman*, based on a play that had triumphed on every stage in Quebec and starring one of the great specialists in whimpering melodrama, Jeanne Demons.

Before I go on to the film itself, I have to come clean and confess that I was jealous of Yvonne Laflamme because she was my age and already making movies. I'd look at her photo in *Radiomonde* and ask myself what she had that I didn't, aside from being a girl.... *Aurore, la petite enfant martyre*, had made her a star, now she was Quebec's favourite child (as my mother put it so well, "It's true you want to spank her, so you can console her afterwards.") and everyone who'd seen the child martyr eating a slice of bread and soap, toasting her little hands on the stove and searing her cheek with an iron wondered what torments could await her in *Coeur de maman*.

I was positive I could play abused children too and there were times (I swear this is the truth) when I'd skip school to go and stand at the door of the Radio-Canada building, at the corner of Dorchester and Bishop, just in case "they" urgently needed some young virgin talent.... I could already picture the scene: Gaétane Laniel, who played all the little boys' parts on the radio, would take sick, "they" had to replace her in "Jeunesse dorée" or some other saga, "they" emerged from the studios totally desperate—and there I was, standing on the corner, free and available. I'd ask, "Do you need somebody?" "They" would reply, "Yes, yes, right away, they're waiting for you in the studio, it's just about noon, 'Les joyeux troubadours' is nearly over, the 'Jeunesse dorée' cast is waiting for you!" I was brilliant of course and "they" were at my feet because I'd saved their lives. No more Gaétane Laniel, three cheers for Michel Rathier (my mother's maiden name, which I'd chosen as my stage name long ago) or Michel d'Entremont, because of the pianist Philippe Entremont—the "de" to make it sound more chic, less working class.

And when I saw Yvonne Laflamme play a little page-boy in Anouilh's *Antigone* on television, next to Thérèse Cadorette and Jean Gascon, I'd thought "they" really had no flair at all. To have a mute boy played by a girl! I ask you! I couldn't believe that "they" hadn't been able to find a little boy who could stand at attention next to Creon while he was yelling at his niece! "They" just had to call me! And meanwhile she was the star, time was passing and I'd soon be too old to play child martyrs or little page-boys in French plays.

So Yvonne Laflamme was in *Coeur de maman*. And since it was a "show for the whole family," I decided to go and check her out.

Coeur de maman was playing at the newly renovated Saint-Denis theatre (this was a few years before the Champlain was redone) and everybody was talking about the incredible luxury of the theatre where the seats sank down *on their own* when you sat in them! I pictured a deep velvet sofa I could flop onto the way I did in front of the television, on three kitchen chairs.

Actually they didn't sink down, they slid back and I felt as if I were lying on my back before the screen, with a very unpleasant sensation between my shoulders, like when you've done some physical exercise (need I add that already I hated physical exercise?) and the muscles in your neck tighten into a painful knot. But it was true that the theatre itself was magnificent.

The audience, a small one now, in the early afternoon, consisted mainly of housewives who'd heard that it was very sad and had come to have a good cry. One lady sat down near me, saying very loud to her friend: "They say it's so sad you go through three hankies at least!" Then took out a pile of white handkerchiefs, very white, very carefully ironed. "Want one? Here, take a couple, you never know...." "No, no, that's all right, I've got my own...."

What struck me first about *Coeur de maman* was the poverty of the music. Accustomed to the syrupy, often thunderous musical magma in American and French movies, I was first surprised, then irritated by the wheezing organ that punctuated every dramatic action very un-subtly. It was so present, I was sure it was hidden in a corner of the set and that we'd eventually see it. Léo Lesieur would realize he was in the shot and he'd bend down abruptly, like TV technicians when they inadvertently find themselves in front of a camera. (I'll never forget the TV version of Oscar Wilde's *Lady Windermere's Fan* in the late fifties: London at the turn of the century. Monique Lepage is expecting company. The company is announced. She makes her way to the doors of her salon, opens them. And there stands the stage manager, glued to the spot, earphones on his head, a stunned look on his face.) But I quickly forgot the awful music, I was so caught up in the "exciting" story.

The screenplay of *Coeur de maman* was worthy of the worst melodramatic Italian tearjerkers of the time, starring Amedeo Nazzari and Yvonne Sanson: a poor mother-in-law (Jeanne Demons) who is abused by her wicked English-Canadian daughter-in law (Roseanna Seaborn), a weak and spineless son (Jean-Paul Kingsley), an adorable granddaughter (guess who). All steeped in an obsessive religiosity (the son and daughter-in-law are the hypocritical owners of a shop that sells pious objects) and a sado-masochism that was a direct offshoot of our finest Judaeo-Christian tradition.

The daughter-in-law was presented at the outset as the wicked woman in all her splendor: besides being an Anglo, she sold rosaries to francophones at ten times what they were worth, if you can imagine! And with an accent you could cut with a knife! But at the very beginning of the film, in a sequence I thought was hilarious, she was put in her place by one of the great Quebec idols at the time: Rose Ouellette herself. Our very own folksy singing star who went by the stage name La Poune, in a cameo greeted by the audience with shouts of joy and liberating laughter, came in to buy something or other, I forget what, a statue of the Virgin I think, and in her own personal slang told the wicked Anglo exactly what she thought of her. A triumph! The lady next to me was already blowing her nose, but with pleasure.

Without going into detail about the plot, I'll just say that it revolved around the fact that the horrible daughter-in-law treated her sweet mother-in-law like a servant: she dressed her up like a maid and made her serve tea (the drawer of water?) when company came to call—the parish priest for instance, already played by Paul Desmarteaux who later on would make a career of it in the TV series *Les belles histoires des pays d'en haut*. The priest befriended the poor woman, not knowing she was the martyred mother of one of the most pious members of his flock, the owner of the shop that sold pious objects, churchwarden, Knight of Columbus, obviously honest—but married to an Anglo, the traitor! But it all worked out in the end because the sweet Denyse Saint-Pierre, yes her, playing some niece or other, discovered what was going on with her dearest friend, the sprightly Jean-Paul Dugas, went to see the future Curé Labelle and tell him everything, while poor Jeanne Demons, driven from her son's house once again, tried to make firewood by rolling up wet newspaper which she put in the oven to dry out. It sounds a little confused but we followed it with passionate interest.

I'd been struck by one sequence in particular: Jeanne Demons, who earlier had been banished from the house by the wicked Anglo because she'd spilled a cup of tea, comes back like a beaten dog, toting a little suitcase, a little black felt hat sitting squarely on her head (we may be poor, but we're clean!). She's soaked to the bones because it's raining very hard. So can you believe that the horrible Roseanna Seaborn refuses to even let her mother-in-law put her suitcase on the floor? The poor woman quivers, shivers and staggers, but the Anglo won't be moved and keeps saying, with her ugly English accent: "Don't put that suitcase on my rug!" I was outraged! I squirmed in my seat amid protests from the audience who wanted to lynch the bitch, I wanted to go because I hated her so much and I was afraid I wouldn't survive her wicked deeds, but I still wanted to know how it was going to end.... Unable to really shower Roseanna Seaborn with the insults she deserved because I had trouble speaking out in public, I merely turned to the woman next to me who was screaming her lungs out and told her shyly: "You're absolutely right!"

When he learned the truth the priest humiliated Roseanna Seaborn during a sequence that provoked a fit of collective hysteria in the audience the like of which I've rarely seen in the movies: keenly felt "Hooray"s on all sides, applause, even some catcalls. A patriotic wind was blowing over the theatre, the Anglo was finally put in her place, banished, cursed!

With the Anglo woman humiliated, the honest son confessed his sins, his weakness, (if I'd been Jeanne Demons I'd have given him a good smack upside the head!) asked forgiveness of his mother who granted it, the idiot, and it all ended with Yvonne Laflamme (having suffered a head injury earlier, through her mother's fault, another twist in the plot!) singing the title song: "O mother's heart, O tender heart, we love you!" amid general euphoria, again accompanied by Léo Lesieur at the organ.

Like the rest of the audience I'd been with the movie all the way, wiping my runny nose and the tears that poured down my face on my short-sleeved summer shirt, thinking Jean-Paul Kingsley was a real asshole, Jeanne Demons too good to be true, restraining myself from telling off the wicked one—unlike the woman next to me who was not too shy to keep jumping up and yelling: "Goddamn cow!" "You make me puke!" and other compliments of the kind. She literally wrung her tear-stained handkerchiefs and often made the gesture of punching the screen as if she personally had something against it for making her cry like that.

As for Yvonne Laflamme, to my great dismay she was excellent. Cute, in character, not too melodramatic (unlike Jeanne Demons, who laid it on thick and then shoveled on some more, in that sickly style that loves suffering so much you wanted to smack her) and she sang her song at the end very prettily, with disarming naturalness. Her presence in the film was refreshing. The very opposite of the monstrous Shirley Temple I could never tolerate, of whom my mother always said: "She's so pretty I could bite her till she bleeds!"

I left the theatre relieved that Roseanne Seaborn had been punished. I think she even died in a traffic accident (my mother and my aunt would have said that "the moral's a good one"), probably to make way for a genuine Québécoise wife in the life of her ever-so-exciting husband. But I was quite depressed that Yvonne Laflamme was so good. With that talent she could go on playing little girls *and even little boys* for a while yet, as I languished with jealousy at the corner of Dorchester and Bishop. I knew now that "they" would never come running out of Radio-Canada onto the sidewalk like chickens with their heads cut off, in search of a great talent: Yvonne Laflamme would take over from Gaétane Laniel!

Back home, I ran straight to my aunt Robertine who was taking out the water tray from under the icebox.

"Get out your pennies, Auntie, and go to the Saint-Denis! You won't be sorry, believe me!"

Twenty Thousand Leagues Under the Sea

This story is about a movie I didn't see in Montreal when it first came out. Here's why.

Like every other North American kid in the fifties, I watched Disney World religiously every week. I'd bought the coonskin cap with the tail that hung down the back of my neck and I followed the adventures of Davy Crockett with a passion, singing that goddamn song our parents swore at; dressed in my Zorro costume and emboldened by my pasted-on mustache, I spent hours tracing Zs with my rubber-tipped tin sword. I dreamed of the day when Disneyland would finally open its doors (I didn't care where California was, I was going there!) I watched, fascinated, as flowers burst into bloom thanks to a new process invented by my idol's good fairies, which let them show in a few seconds what took minutes, hours, days to happen: roses growing to the sound of Tchaikovsky's "Waltz of the Flowers" and the sun setting like an orange dropping into the sea.

Then, over the course of one whole season, Walt Disney kept me on tenterhooks with the making of a film that promised images and adventures the likes of which had never before been seen as he said himself and he should know: *Twenty Thousand Leagues Under the Sea*, in Technicolor and Cinemascope, starring Kirk Douglas,

James Mason and Peter Lorre. Not a week went by that Walt didn't show us and describe the mysterious lights under the sea that frighten all the sailors in the world, the diving bells built precisely according to the descriptions in Jules Verne's book, the wood-paneled cabin of the evil Captain Nemo where Kirk Douglas and his crew, grappling with the famous giant octopus would, we were told in a terrifying voice, turn the hair of all us Pablum-fed youngsters prematurely white.

The scene with the octopus I saw dozens of times, first in little bits and then complete: during shooting, in preparation, a simple sketch.... There were interviews with the director, the actors (Kirk Douglas still in his sailor's cap saying it was the most difficult scene he'd ever had to film, while Peter Lorre looked on with his usual big round eyes), the critter's designers explained how it worked and the artists who'd added the finishing touches showed us how disgusting the tentacles and suckers were. We saw how a storm is produced in a studio and we even knew how many gallons of water were used.... This went on for weeks and left viewers asking for more. It was probably shameless self-promotion but we poor dupes didn't realize that, on the contrary we were thrilled to have the privilege of seeing entire scenes before the movie came out. Thanks again, Uncle Walt!

We were told to watch the papers, to keep an eye on the cinema marquees, it was coming, it was not to be missed, and children in particular were going to be indulged like never before! And never before had I looked forward to a film so much! I dreamed about it, I ate it, I thought about nothing else; I bugged my friend Réal who had no interest in adventure stories whatsoever and thought I was a pain in the neck, I'd read the book five times to be sure I'd understand everything, because the first copies of the film that came to Montreal were sure to be in English: in other words I was so well prepared I felt as if I'd already seen it!

Every night when my brother Jacques came home with *La Presse* I grabbed the paper and opened it to the Entertainment section, hoping to see a big ad for *Twenty Thousand Leagues Under the Sea* that said it was coming soon. A quarter-page, a half-page, why not: Kirk Douglas, James Mason, Peter Lorre, the evil octopus, the Nautilus, the deep-sea divers in…. I'd run to the theatre and it would be the best movie I'd ever seen!

But on the day the ad finally appeared I wanted to die.

First I felt the adrenaline rush that shakes you up when you're surprised or overexcited. There was the ad, as big as I'd hoped! The film was opening the following Friday! Just three more days and I could see it at last!

I remember I'd spread the paper on the kitchen floor in front of the stove and I was practically lying down on the ad, I was so worked up.

But…something was missing. Actually I'd noticed it right away, but I didn't want to know it so I went on playing happy for fear of plunging too quickly into despair. I procrastinated. I shilly-shallied….

It wasn't a "show for the whole family!" There was nothing in the ad that said I could go to the Loew's next Friday. I was stunned.

They'd lied to me! Walt Disney himself had lied to me! For months! He'd held out an inaccessible mirage and made me think I could have it! And all that time he'd been putting the finishing touches on a film for adults!

I prepared my outburst very carefully. I waited till everyone was there, except my father of course, who worked nights, and it was a brilliant performance. By that I don't mean I wasn't sincere, I was, but I was aware of my sincerity, I was even a spectator of it and I was enjoying the act I was putting on as much as I was suffering from the underlying pain. Maybe to protect myself from the *true* outburst, the one by which I could have damned my soul, that I was holding back because it scared me, whereas this one, when you get right down to it, was more like a temper tantrum by a spoiled brat who wants to see a movie that's not intended for him.

Which was how the rest of the family seemed to interpret the incident, with a grain of salt. Not me. I'd been cheated, it was unfair and I demanded restitution. I would write to Walt Disney, I'd shower him with insults, he'd be so ashamed he'd apologize before the whole world, all thanks to me.... I went to bed feverish, furious, humiliated at having been taken in, at having believed a liar, at having dared to dream.

***

The next morning, I realized right away that my mother had told my father everything because he got up when I did, though he usually slept till ten or eleven.

I thought to myself: that's it, here comes the sermon, even though that wasn't really my father's style. He was serious, nearly pensive; he walked around me while he put in his hearing aid. Over my last slice of toast I told him, almost shouting:

"Go on, say what you've got to say so I'll know how I'm going to be punished after school...."

He seemed surprised. He came and sat down beside me.

"You know, about that *Twenty Thousand Leagues Under the Sea*...that movie you can't go to because it's not for children.... That's because we aren't in the States here. I mean...in the States they don't keep kids out of the movies.... It's only here they do that.... In the States, you can take your kids and I hear you can even smoke in the theatre."

I remembered that my father had followed every step in the development of the movie almost as passionately as I had, and I realized he was probably very disappointed that he couldn't take me. And that he wouldn't go without me out of solidarity. What a letdown for him too! He was condemning himself to not seeing a film because his child couldn't.

But there was a surprise waiting for me.

He poured himself some coffee, put two slices of bread in the toaster.

"Y'know...just across the border...in Plattsburgh, say...they've got drive-ins.... It's the States, so children can go. I talked it over with your mother...you've been bugging us about it.... So we'll ask one of your brothers to take all three of us to see *Twenty Thousand Leagues Under the Sea* this weekend.... If you behave yourself...."

And that morning, in 1955, in North America, a little thirteen-year-old boy dared to contravene the tacit rule that existed between males and he kissed his father on both cheeks.

✳✳✳

As neither of my brothers could drive us to Plattsburgh that weekend, my father fell back on his friends the Martineaus. She worked with him at the printshop, but in the bindery, while my father was a pressman. Her husband drove a monster refrigerated truck that transported fruit from Florida to Quebec. He'd be gone for a week, then home for a week. Madame Martineau used to say they had an alternative marriage: one week on, one week off.

They were very entertaining. Madame Martineau was funny and she adored disguises. She'd usually come to the house dressed like something from Harper's Bizarre, in mismatched multicolored clothes, with a huge hair-ribbon or some grotesque hat sitting crookedly on her head, outrageously made up and always in a bubbly mood. She would burst into the dining room warbling "Tico-Tico," imitating Alys Robi, or singing Carmen Miranda's latest hit, trying out a few dance steps, always the same ones, then collapsing into the rocking chair with a laugh.

My mother said: "You didn't get out of your car decked out like that, I hope!" and Madame Martineau replied: "No, Madame Tremblay, I was in a lot worse shape than this!"

If the two couples went out together, Madame Martineau would go into the bathroom and fix herself up a little, too little for my mother's liking, actually, which led her to say that people had stared at them all evening and it was her fault, the clown. If they stayed home to play cards or watch the hockey game on TV, she wouldn't change a thing in her appearance and spent the evening laughing at her oversized jewellery or her lavish bracelets.

Madame Martineau looked a little like Betty Hutton and I think she knew it.

My mother claimed she was in love with my father (her husband was very ugly and she was rather abrupt with him), and called her "his sweetie from the shop," which seemed to flatter him because he never protested.

So on the morning in question Madame Martineau arrived disguised as Captain Nemo, or what she thought Captain Nemo would look like: white pants, sailor's jacket, sailor's cap, dark glasses—and a beard drawn on with burnt cork. Her husband called her his ducky little sailor-boy, pinching her rear as he said it. She cooed, saying: "Oh no, sir, I don't go with men!" I had a good laugh at her act. My mother didn't.

"Go wash off that beard, you look ridiculous. As if you'd dunked your chin in tar."

Madame Martineau saluted.

"At your orders, Admiral."

And disappeared into the bathroom.

My mother looked as if she thought the day was getting off to a bad start, while Monsieur Martineau, my father and I were more inclined to be thrilled at the great adventure that was about to begin.

Madame Martineau came out with a clean chin, but she'd blackened one eye as if she'd got into a fight in the bathroom.

Her husband gave a hollow laugh.

"Wipe that off, everybody'll think I beat you."

She looked him straight in the eye.

"If only you did beat me!"

I didn't understand what that meant but I could see that everyone but Madame Martineau was uncomfortable.

✶✶✶

Monsieur Martineau and my father sat in front, the women and I in the back. The men gabbed, loudly, because they were both hard of hearing, the women gabbed, loudly, to make themselves heard over their husbands; while I kept craning my neck so I could see everything. My father didn't have a car and we rarely left Montreal.

The sun was setting when we drove across the Jacques Cartier Bridge. Ahead of us, the sky was the dark blue that heralded night; behind it, the sun was settling into a bed of pink and orange clouds. I knelt on the seat and watched the glorious spectacle through the framework of the bridge. Montreal was silhouetted in black against the sunset, reminding me of the paint-by-numbers sets my mother was so fond of and consumed in impressive quantities. The walls of the house were being covered over with Mona Lisas whose smiles didn't quite make it, with South Sea storms and garish tropical sunsets.

We drove through Ville Jacques-Cartier where my maternal grandmother lived (my mother: "This is the first time in years I've crossed the bridge without going to see Ma..."), then we headed due south in the direction of the United States.

I'd never been out of the country before and the mere thought of going through customs had me quaking. My brothers had told me that soldiers armed to the teeth would ask us for our papers, ("Better take your baptismal certificate or you could end up in Sing Sing!") then they'd probably search us even in our most intimate areas to see if we were concealing weapons, cigarettes or drugs. I didn't see how we could conceal cigarettes, weapons or drugs in our intimate areas, but even so I was scared.

I was quite nervous then when we drove up to the customs officer. Especially because Madame Martineau hadn't bothered to get rid of her phony black eye.

But there was a surprise in store: Monsieur Martineau knew the customs officer, who seemed glad to see him. They exchanged a few jokes, laughing too loud, I realized my father's friend was introducing his wife as his sister, probably because of that black eye, then he pointed to us and claimed he was going to the States to take back some rotten fruit the stores had turned down. The American gave him a friendly tap on the shoulder, waving him through and calling him a frog.

Smugly, Monsieur Martineau swelled his chest with pride.

"They're all my pals, those guys.... They're okay...."

His wife had turned around.

"You should introduce me to them..."

✶✶✶

My first drive-in was pretty tacky. A paved entrance with no greenery, a parking lot studded with listening posts that looked like out-of-commission parking metres, damaged screens, projection that left something to be desired. But we were all excited anyway: we were in the States, it was a fine evening and we were going to see a movie outdoors.

Madame Martineau watched what was going on in the other cars, giving my mother knowing looks. She pointed to kissing couples.

"There'll be steam rising in that car before long, that's for sure!"

My mother gave her a tap on the hand.

"Madame Martineau, the boy...."

"Well, let him look and learn.... He'll soon be making the steam rise himself, he might as well know what to do...."

She leaned forward in her husband's direction.

"Is this where you bring your American chicks?"

He had no need to answer, his guilty look said it all. Madame Martineau made a sound that was supposed to be a laugh but was closer to pain.

We had to suffer through a bad black-and-white thriller before it got really dark and they finally showed *Twenty Thousand Leagues Under the Sea.*

My father turned towards me.

"Come sit in the front, you'll see better."

Already the magical name of Walt Disney was being written across the screen.

∗∗∗

What a letdown.

They'd shown the best parts on TV a hundred times: the Nautilus like a big phosphorescent fish, the stupid octopus that in the end wasn't very realistic, Captain Nemo's aquarium cabin, the metal diving bells, the storm that on the big screen just looked like special effects. The rest was English babbling I couldn't understand a word of. Close-ups of Kirk Douglas, Peter Lorre and James Mason who carried on endlessly about scientific matters. Bo-ring. Even the colour didn't add much: it was all greenish, yellow and brown. The novel was infinitely more filmic and I had a kind thought for Jules Verne who'd invented cinematic cutting before the film-makers. And an unkind one for Walt Disney, who had cheated me shamefully once again. They'd promised me an hour and a half of rapture and delivered a padded-out trailer.

We'd come all this way for nothing and I felt guilty. I'd led four adults into a pointless adventure and I wanted to apologize but didn't have the guts.

Besides that, Monsieur Martineau was starting to smell of sweat.

The two women had very quickly fallen asleep. Madame Martineau was snoring softly. My father had put his arm around my shoulders. My eyes were heavy, I was struggling against sleep. I barely heard him tell me: "It doesn't matter if you go to sleep, it's pretty boring," before I dropped into my own version of *Twenty Thousand Leagues Under the Sea*, which was certainly more interesting, far more colorful at any rate, closer to the wild animated drawings of *Cinderella* I'd loved so much than to the dull psychological drama we were looking at now.

***

I never knew what time we arrived back home, or in what state, or if the film got any better near the end, because we never mentioned it again. And we never went to another drive-in.

The Mighty Joe Brown

The very first movie I ever saw, when I was five or six, was a horror film. It left its mark.

My brothers, especially Bernard, devotedly went to the movies at the St. Stanislas parish hall, immortalized by Robert Charlebois in his song "Fu-Manchu" and which I've spoken about at length myself in *The Duchess and the Commoner*; I won't say much about it now, then, except to point out that the children from Plateau Mont-Royal used to pile in there every Saturday afternoon, the boys for the one o'clock screening, the girls for the one at three, and to the accompaniment of an inextricable tangle of shuffling chairs, shouting, wild racing and flinging of paper, we watched second-rate movies that were mostly in English and rarely in colour.

My brothers and my girl cousins were of course no exception. They devoured everything with the same joy: the animated cartoon, the feature, the serial that always ended badly, which they'd discuss the end of all the next week while speculating on the intelligence of the bad guys and the naiveté of the good.... But the boys always saw everything before the girls did, which had its advantages: at the end of the one o'clock showing, my brother Bernard, the less serious of the two and an incorrigible joker, would race out of the hall and head straight for Jeanne, Lise and Hélène who were waiting in line, chattering away, and tell them if it was worth seeing or not; sometimes he'd go into too much detail about what he'd just seen and they'd send him away, yelling and plugging their ears, especially if he'd dared say anything about the serial. They wanted to know whether or not the good guy had been blown up with the bomb when he landed in the ravine with the flaming stagecoach drawn by racing horses, but they didn't want to hear it from him. If he had liked the film a lot he'd even try to sneak in to the second showing, but the boys weren't allowed in without a letter duly signed by a parent so he was inevitably turned down.

***

For that afternoon they'd announced a kind of bargain basement *King Kong* entitled *The Mighty Joe Brown*, with a man in a monkey costume trying to pass himself off as a big bad gorilla that murdered women in a large American city, Chicago or New York, I can't remember which, entering their houses through the window. And that was the day Bernard had got it in his head to introduce me to the movies, a shrewd choice for a sadist (I never got him to admit whether he'd chosen that one deliberately or if it was just coincidence), but disastrous in any case because you don't take a child who's never seen a movie in his life to watch a gorilla come in people's windows to disembowel them.

I remember just one thing from that afternoon, just one image that comes back to me fairly often, even forty years later, because it was certainly one of the most intense, most violent moments in my life.

It is night, a woman is sleeping on her back. Next to her bed, an open window. Can you guess what's coming? The wind stirs the curtains very gently, the shadow of a tree-branch is swaying. The worst horror film cliché but a totally innocent image for a child who's never seen a movie and has no idea what's coming next. I'm sitting on the edge of my wooden chair, moving it to make it squeak because I'm finding the film supremely boring and I'm watching the screen with one rather distracted eye. Bernard has told me where to look—at the big piece of white cloth that's about to start moving, saying it's going to be terrific even if it's in English—but nothing I've seen so far is the least bit interesting. The only thing that bothers me is to wonder how they've got rid of the colours of the walls, the bed, the curtains, the characters (don't forget I don't even know what a movie is, so this is the first time I've even seen black and white) and I'm about to ask my brother. But now something is attracting my attention. Did I really see a shadow at the window? My heart stops. A shot of the woman, still asleep, perfectly trusting, perfectly beautiful in her slumber. The hall has fallen silent: I'm not the only one who suspects something. I've stopped making my chair squeak. Again! This time I'm sure. There's something, somebody behind that window, maybe swinging on the tree branch that keeps innocently swaying back and forth.... Somebody stocky, heavy, because the silhouette is all bent over. Unless it's a monster crouching down to look small, the better to make its leap! I'm about to tug at my brother's sleeve, ask if he saw the same thing I did, when the curtains part as the woman stirs and turns onto her stomach.

Horror, indescribable!

A gorilla twice the size of a man enters the bedroom without a sound and bends over the woman's bed.

The whole world collapses. I'm nothing but an open mouth, a strident cry, the very expression of fear. I'm on my feet, stiff as a poker, and I'm screaming. The rest of the audience has screamed too, but I keep it up after the others, after the scene has ended, after the woman in the film has fainted at the sight of the gorilla that's about to sniff her. I'm convinced that I'll never be able to stop. The other children, all older than me, who have recovered quickly from their moment of terror, who might even be inclined to laugh at it now that it's over, look at me, amused and surprised at first but then they start yelling at me to shut up because they can't hear the show. My brother has slapped his hand over my mouth but I keep it up, trying to bite him. When there's no air left in my lungs, I take a deep breath and start up again, on the same note, with the same intensity. I've changed forever in this world where gorillas get inside your house through the window to strangle you, chop you into little pieces, maybe even eat you, because of course gorillas must be carnivores!

I'm lifted off the floor, carted on Bernard's shoulder amid shouting; I see the rows of children parade before my eyes while the film continues to unfurl on the screen. How can they tolerate such a thing? How can they control their fear, not rise up against that huge animal who I'm sure is going to eat that poor woman alive? We have to do something, call the police, the fire department, an ambulance!

Outside on the sidewalk I'm still crying; the girls who have started to form a line on Laurier frown as they watch us go past. Bernard reassures my cousin Jeanne, telling her I'm too young, the film isn't all that scary....

The trouble is that I keep screaming after we're back home.

***

While my brother didn't get smacked, he did get a strip torn off him.

My mother: "At least you could've told me it was a scary movie, you idiot! Take a child his age to see naked women being visited by gorillas in their bedroom! It could mark him for life! He sleeps by the window, do you know what he'll think about when he goes to bed, will you tell me? He'll see monkeys everywhere, for one thing. And who do you think's going to have to console him in the middle of the night, eh? Not you, you sleep like a log, you wouldn't notice if your ear was hit by lightning! If he starts wetting his bed again because he's been traumatized you'll be the one that washes his sheets! And let me tell you something else: there'll be bananas growing on coconut trees on St. Joseph Boulevard—and monkeys too—before you go back to that parish hall! And the rest of them, the people that show you those movies, what are they thinking about? Do they know they can mess you up for life by showing you things like that?"

She rocked me a little too hard while she was yelling at my brother and I felt sick to my stomach. Which stopped me from screaming any more. Now that I couldn't get rid of my terror by howling, I whimpered like a teething baby.

It was long, violent, dramatic. Bernard had been taken down a notch or two, my mother's voice had gone up a notch or two, and the neighbours were all ears.

I cried for a long time, my mother shouted for a long time and at ten o'clock mass the next morning, everybody was looking at her, she said later, as if she was a monstress who mistreated her own children.

As for me, needless to say I spent a terrible night, populated with gorillas in black and white that took great delight in my fear. The more frightened I was, the surer I was that I could see them snickering, amused at my cries, my lamentations, my pleading, their beady little eyes damp with joy, their lips curled in a hideous grimace, their powerful teeth ready to plant themselves in my own frail little neck.

***

It was a long time before I could go back to the movies after that disastrous adventure. And when I did return to the St. Stanislas parish hall, I went in secret, with ten cents I'd accumulated a penny at a time by depriving myself of Marie-Sylvia's surprise bags or milk at morning recess. I begged my brothers not to give me away, but in any case they were starting to lose interest in these children's shows and let me do as I wanted; sometimes they even lent me the money.

***

But I sometimes wonder now if my great passion for bad horror films (I've seen everything the Americans have produced since the fifties and for years I'd run to see the Hammer films with Peter Cushing and Christopher Lee) doesn't come from that first movie experience, even though it was so traumatic. Behind the absolute terror experienced by a child who can't understand what he's seeing, perhaps there was, ultimately, a tiny shudder of pleasure, very close to orgasmic, that I've been able to control as I've got older and that I like to experience again in a darkened theatre. Because when I'm frightened in the movies, I really am afraid, and I enjoy it—a lot! (When I saw *Alien*, in 1979, I was so terrified I had acute indigestion when I left the theatre and then I went back the next day to see how it was done.) And if a film is bad, I have a different kind of pleasure, but pleasure all the same!

Fifties Horror Films

During a good part of my adolescence the Princess theatre, now the Parisien, every week ran two horror films or low-budget science fiction features which I savored with boundless pleasure, a bag of Maple Leaf chips and a large Coke.

On Friday afternoon, with school over for the week, I'd take the Amherst trolley bus to St. Catherine Street, then the streetcar to the theatre. I set out from the corner of Laurier and De la Roche because I was attending St. Stanislas secondary school, concentrating in science. Don't ask me what I was doing there, I don't know either. I'd get off at the corner of University (Montreal was still an English city), retrace my steps, go past the System where I'd never ventured because of its unsavory reputation (it was said that abominations went on in the toilets that were worthy of Sodom, Gomorrah and Paris). I'd hang around for a while outside the Orpheum where during the theatre season my idols from the Théâtre du Nouveau Monde performed (ah! those posters designed by Normand Hudon that showed Guy Hoffman, Jean Gascon, Monique Leyrac....) then I'd cross the street where the lighted marquee of the Princess advertised some mediocre movie like *I Was A Teenage Werewolf* or *Monster of the Blue Lagoon*, along with some other equally inane feature, my treats for the week, my reward after five days of boredom surrounded by incomprehensible logarithms, the suspicious smells of chemistry experiments and the subtleties dividing formal logic from symbolic logic.

The Princess lobby was immense, long and narrow, with a strong smell of fresh popcorn and melted butter. The first thing I did was pee (I was already known for my tiny bladder) in the "sumptuous" marble washrooms in the basement, where the smell of mothballs mixed with that of urine poorly drained by the always defective system caught at your throat quite unpleasantly. I tried not to breathe while I was there but I never succeeded and I'd run back up the stairs, coughing and grimacing.

And then I was ready for three hours of horrified cries by incompetent actresses with bulging eyes and dyed blonde hair, of poorly executed transformations of bad actors into ridiculous triangle-shaped creatures from outer space or bargain-basement werewolves, of shameless, indecent hamming by John Agar, Vincent Price, Boris Karloff or the loathsome Bela Lugosi—epitome of the failed actor who permanently drags around with him the old torn clothes from his one success, in his case Dracula. "I never drink vvvvine!" is funny once, but not if it's dragged out over an entire career!

I went into the theatre which had its own strong smell, the damp aroma of poorly washed men and poorly digested beer. It was always full to bursting. Every Friday. And the audience was entirely male. No woman would have dared set foot in the theatre at that time of day without feeling a little guilty and lacking in judgment. A self-respecting woman would no more smoke on the street or go to the Princess theatre on Friday night than she'd go to a tavern.

I had trouble finding a seat at the end of a row, where I still like to sit because I know I won't disturb anyone if I have to get up during the movie because of an urgent call of nature.

I usually arrived in the middle of a film, but it didn't matter; I wasn't really there for the story anyway, but rather for the thrill I'd feel at the hand emerging from a wall to strangle someone, or the vampire's fangs sinking into a beautiful, appetizing neck; the poisoned darts of the extraterrestrial that stay in the upper back where you can't reach them; the cat looming out of the alley that you've mistaken for a monster; the Martian vomiting lumpy soup that scalds the skin of poor Earthlings; the giant spider thirsty for fresh blood; the thirty-foot tall woman who tramples everything, but not on purpose; the idiot; the shrunken man who has to fight a cat with a knitting needle; the bat that foreshadows Dracula; the obvious hypocrisy of Igor—the mad doctor's eternal assistant, servile and treacherous; or the Prince of Darkness himself, come to earth for a harvest of feeble souls—the always ugly, always humpbacked Igor who invariably dies an atrocious death to applause and "Hurray"s from the audience. I was part of it and I was taking part!

As for the thrills, I had plenty.

***

I knew though that most of the time, those films were bad. I was beginning to understand what it was that for me meant a film was good or not. My taste was developing. I was learning not only the names of the actors but also those of the directors, I could cite a couple of films by John Ford even if I hadn't seen them, I gladly recounted Carné's *Les Visiteurs du soir* to anyone willing to listen because that film had bowled me over, I rooted around in film magazines which were very rare at the time, but got my attention simply because they had the word "cinéma" or "movie" in their titles.

My horizons were bursting open on all sides. I'd left the children's section at the Municipal Library and registered in the adults', giving me access to all the knowledge in the world; with shivers of excitement I'd moved on from Jules Verne to Dostoevsky, from the children's series "Signes de pistes" to the 19th century French and German romantics, from Tintin to Jack London. I knew of the existence of Proust though I hadn't yet dared to try reading him. I had just discovered Greek theatre and already I was wondering who was right, Agamemnon or Clytemnestra. I was quickly becoming an avid consumer of culture. My taste in music was becoming clearer, in the sense that I was naively beginning to think that Tchaikovsky was tacky and Wagner sublime. I watched four or five hours of television every day. I knew all of Marcel Dubé, Yves Thériault, André Langevin, Françoise Loranger. I read and listened to Félix Leclerc religiously, to the great disapproval of my father who had no use for folksy guitar scrapers and wearers of quaint lumberjack shirts. I'd devoured *The Tin Flute* during a trip to the Gaspé with my parents and I was positive that never again would I read such a beautiful novel. I was reading Tennessee Williams on the sly though I wasn't exactly sure why and I was writing things in the margins of novels by Julien Green. I was carried away by the poetry of Saint-Denys Garneau and that of his cousin, Anne Hébert. I was the only one in the family who didn't laugh at the antics of the ballet dancers on *L'Heure du Concert* on TV. Wednesday nights, I went to the Théâtre du Nouveau Monde and the Comédie canadienne because they had students' tickets for ninety cents. I could only see the top of my idols' heads but I gorged myself on lines by Anouilh as delivered by Ginette Letondal and Robert Gadouas, on the brilliant Molière of Guy Hoffman, on Denise Pelletier's Marguerite in Marcel Dubé's *Le temps des lilas*, on Jean Gascon's doge in *Venise sauvée*, on the imagination of Paul Buissonneau who turned a bad play by Marcel Aymé, *Les oiseaux de lune*, into a magnificent aviary in which Claude Léveillée and Germaine Dugas made their acting debuts.

I worried my father and my brothers because I was too "artistic" and I was the delight of my mother who tried, not always successfully, to take an interest in the same things I did.

So why this sudden infatuation with what was so obviously the very opposite of what I should have liked in the movies?

Over the weeks and months I became aware of something very troubling. I wasn't really going to those movies to be scared. Not just for that, anyway. Something else was attracting me to that dark room where an unsightly mess of all that was ugly in the world was projected to an audience of men who weren't always paying attention: my affinity with the so-called evil or accursèd characters, my sympathy for what I guessed to be their unhappiness—the misunderstood and pariahs of all kinds, often very ugly, who'd been assembled from the scattered pieces of other beings as in *Frankenstein*, or who came from so far away there were no points of comparison and it was easier to see them as evil individuals who wanted to destroy us than as creatures lost in the galaxy who were searching for some hypothetical aid.

The revolt of the creature who turns against his creator and perishes along with him, the confession of the vampire who tells us that for centuries, he's been desperately seeking the rest that is strictly forbidden him, the witch who doesn't want to experience being burned at the stake again, the werewolf who after all isn't responsible for the effects of the full moon on his body hair, the extraterrestrial whose planet has run out of water and who'd like to pump away ours—all those victims of human stupidity or the complexity of the galaxies, who were depicted as monsters of evil, touched me and drew my sympathy.

Even if they often terrified me because of the very structure of the films, which always came down on the side of so-called normality, the situation in which these creatures inevitably found themselves at the end always touched me, and sometimes I'd even wipe away a tear when Christopher Lee was impaled; when the phantom of the opera—epitome of the ugly, rejected lover—perished in the blaze of what had been his lair; or when the woman who'd become a giant because of nuclear fallout exploded amid horrible convulsions, cursing the whole world. I thought I understood them or rather, I think I understood them. And I'd settle in to watch them every Friday, jumping when they seemed about to burst through the screen and strangle me, but also weeping over their disappearance and perpetuating their mourning because it was so unfair that they should die. I hated Dr. Frankenstein, finding him pretentious when he took himself for God, and I sympathized with his creature because it was irresponsible and innocent.

That, obviously, was something else I kept to myself, the audience at the Princess theatre between five and eight on Friday night being more apt to noisily applaud the death of Dracula than to take pity on the fate of a naïve and wretched victim.

***

I would emerge from the theatre groggy, happy and famished.

I'd get home around half-past eight and my mother would be at the end of the table waiting for me. My father worked from four p.m. till midnight so he was rarely there in the evening, and when he was it meant he'd lost his job or been laid off, so that I preferred it if he wasn't there when I returned from the movies; my brother Bernard was already married and Jacques had gone out to do what young men in their twenties do on Friday night. So I'd be alone with my mother who would dish up a generous helping of beans or eggs goldenrod before going back to her place at the end of the table.

My mother hated fish and she'd decided that the rest of us did too so she wouldn't have to cook it on meatless Fridays. Her repertoire was very limited then and we nearly always ate the same thing, envying the children of my aunt Marguerite who stuffed themselves with haddock fillets, fish-sticks, scallops and even shrimp, lucky them! As for us, after the inevitable vegetable soup (there was always a pot of it simmering on my mother's stove—you might have thought it was the same one which she kept endlessly stretching out, one she'd started the day after her wedding and that wouldn't cool down till she died), it was the inevitable beans, delicious but they turned up too often for my liking; the eggs goldenrod that I hated more than anything; or the toasted tomato sandwiches my mother fixed in no time when she didn't feel like making anything else.

When I'd finished my dessert I'd pour myself a cup of coffee, turn down the sound on the TV which we'd set up next to the dining-room table, the heart of the house, and tell her about what I'd just seen. In detail. She'd rest her elbows on the tablecloth, cup her chin in her hands so they framed her cheeks, and smile. She heard it all: the decapitations, the witches burned at the stake, the death of Igor, the impalement of Christopher Lee, the triangular monsters with poisoned needles at their fingertips, the flying saucers that destroyed entire cities with a single ray; punctuating my account with little cries of disgust, with "ttt"s of discouragement, with, "For heaven's sake!", with "What a disgusting thing to do!", with "Stop, you just ate, you'll make yourself sick, telling me things like that!"—but never did she seriously ask me to break off my story. She knew how it all would wind up just as I had in the theatre, but she listened till the end, just as I'd watched the film till it was over, drinking in my words, in agony when the heroine descended the stairs to the cellar, terrified when Peter Cushing violated Dracula's tomb, relieved when Evil was vanquished, defeated by the always triumphant Good.

Then she would sigh and add: "The moral's a good one," and get out of her chair to clean up and do the dishes. Sometimes, when I settled down in front of the TV to watch some late-night show, she'd shout at me from the kitchen: "Too bad I hate those movies, or I'd go with you...."

I pictured my mother in the theatre full of men, I tried to guess how she'd react, I promised myself to take her, one of these days.... But I suppose my descriptions were all she needed, because she never saw a horror movie in her life, not even on television.

The King and I

On the day I turned fourteen, June 26, 1956, I decided that from now on I was going to go to movies with the adults, even though I didn't meet the age requirement. I'd had enough of animated cartoons, lives of saints, edifying melodramas or Heidi coming down from her mountain to take care of a little cripple in town. I wanted to see Susan Hayward in her strapless gowns, Lana Turner in her fuzzy sweaters, Marilyn Monroe lying in her Niagara Falls. At the time I wasn't very interested in French films, I saw too many on television, and I was getting sick of Fernandel's faces, Georges Guétary's quavery voice and the tralala of Suzy Delair.

At the Palace theatre they were advertising a musical comedy entitled *The King and I* which I'd never heard of but which immediately grabbed my attention: in the ad in *La Presse*, a beautiful woman wearing a wide satin gown was dancing in the arms of what appeared to be a half-naked Indo-Chinese man. That was all I needed to make up my mind and I set out with pounding heart to mount an assault on a movie theatre that had the reputation of being invincible if you were under sixteen.

I hadn't yet made the mistake of my brother Bernard who'd drawn on a mustache once to get into the Passe-Temps with our aunt Robertine, only to be met with the cashier's laughter. She'd regretted her action as a matter of fact when my father's sister decided to come to her nephew's defense with her stentorian voice and her flowery language. On Mont-Royal Street people were still talking about it. No, I was dressed simply: blue pants, short-sleeved white shirt, red V-neck, my Pat Boone shoes. I probably looked like a cartoon version of a real little gentleman.

From my window on the St. Catherine Street tramway I could see the ad for the film, the same one but in colour, and my courage failed me. If besides asking me my age, the cashier demanded some ID...if she called the police ...if I landed in jail because I'd wanted to see a film that, in the end, was really too "adult" for me.... I stayed on for a few stops and got off at Ogilvy's. It was barely ten-thirty a.m. (the first showing was at eleven) and I was already sweating. I walked back as far as Eaton's, across the street from the Palace, and stood on tiptoe to try and see what the cashier looked like.... Impossible, needless to say. I crossed the street, avoiding the cars and streetcars that were coming in tight ranks in both directions.

She didn't look particularly easy-going. I pretended to be checking out the photos—which were very beautiful actually, glossy and sharp and made you want to see the damn film even more—while I kept glancing furtively towards the glass cage. The cashier was old, fat, serious, and she handed out the tickets like some rare and precious manna, gesturing broadly and staring hard at the customer. She wasn't there to enjoy herself and she let you know it.

Did that mean I was sentenced to another two years of Heidi and her goat and her fat neighbour?

Deciding I'd been standing there too long, the cashier took a coin and started rapping it against her glass cage, gesturing to me to move on. I must have looked like a depraved child who stands around in front of dirty

111

pictures so I took off, my shoulders hunched and my tail between my legs.

It was a quarter to eleven and my birthday was already ruined.

I needed consolation.

I darted into Eaton's and headed straight for the record department on the fifth floor.

∗∗∗

At that time you could buy classical recordings on the Remington and Plymouth labels for the huge sum of ninety-nine cents. They all sounded equally bad and had probably been recorded in studios the size of match-boxes, but I made do with them because I didn't know anything else, my budget being, to say the least, limited. I already owned a fairly impressive collection, basics like the inevitable suites from *Carmen* or *Peer Gynt* and excerpts from *Swan Lake*, but also some works that were less obvious for a neophyte of fourteen—Bruch's violin concerto, for instance, or Stravinsky's *Pulcinella*. I also had Mozart's *Cosi* sung by second-rate German singers with flowery names like Elsie Plümaacher, whose Italian sounded hilarious. But I didn't mind, I was learning, I liked everything, I thought it was all sublime, I cried like a calf over Saint-Saëns' ballet music for *Samson and Delilah* as much as over the first chorus of Bach's *St. John Passion*.

I was going then to work off my frustration and for another twenty-four cents, buy a fine classical recording that would bring me dozens and dozens of hours of listening instead of the hypothetical pleasure of watching the lady in the long dress dance with the half-bare-naked Siamese man. Obviously I'd decided that *The King and I* wasn't worth risking jail for and that, in any event, it would probably bore me to death.

Eaton's record department had listening booths for customers where I'd already spent quite a lot of time choosing among three or four records, often unable to make up my mind; I was known there and the salesladies liked me because I was probably their only teenage customer who bought something besides the records of Patti Page or Gale Storm.

That morning though I was out of luck, there was a new girl at the cash register whom I seemed to be disturbing, so much did she look as if she wanted to be somewhere else.

And our conversation got off to a very bad start.

"Could you open this record for me please, I'd like to listen to it."

She looked at me as if I were a dog turd on a velvet cushion.

"Sorry, I don't speak French."

I knew it was store policy for people to speak English but there was no way that girl was an Anglo, absolutely no way! The accent, the face, the hairdo, the clothes, the gum—it was all straight from the Plateau Mont-Royal or the Faubourg à mélasse. She was a carbon copy of my cousin Lise who worked next door at Kresge's, who used to tell us how people would order a cheese sandwich in English and she'd bring them a ham sandwich in French...and that most of all, nobody was going to make her speak English if she didn't feel like it! Except that the Eaton's salesgirl had decided to play the game.

She wasn't much older than I was, she was a long way from twenty in any event, and I decided to stand up to her.

"Don't make me laugh, you're as French as I am.... Anyway, I don't want a conversation, I just want you to open this record...."

She raised her eyebrows in circumflex accents and shook her head. And in her best English accent came out with an "I beg your pardon," that emerged from her lips like the most elegant *joual*.

I couldn't help laughing.

"Look, make a little effort, okay, I know you aren't English so why keep trying?"

The salesgirl leaned across the counter towards me.

"What the hell do you want, you little creep, you want me lose my job?"

She glanced furtively to her right and pretended she was busy at the cash register.

Near the escalators, some manager or other was watching us suspiciously, not even bothering to hide his dismal performance as an underpaid spy out to catch in *flagrante delicto* two francophones who were communicating in their language. I got the picture in an instant: the constant humiliations, the harassment, the small and pitiful capitulations. I felt sorry for her. And for me.

"Okay, pretend I talked English to you. He didn't hear us."

I felt like an asshole. So did she.

She ripped the cellophane off the record sleeve and held it out with an extremely stupid look on her face.

"Think you're smart, eh? Just wait till you're in my shoes!"

As I headed for the listening booth I came across the record of *The King and I* in the place of honour on the display racks. I picked it up, looked at it from every angle. It looked fantastic!

Of course I wanted to listen to it. On my way back to the cash register to have it opened, I noticed the spy who'd come to stand next to the salesgirl, smiling ferociously as he watched me come back. They weren't going to make me speak English with them! When I got to the counter I showed the salesgirl the record, totally ignoring the manager, I tore the cellophane myself with my thumb the way I'd seen her do with the other record, then I turned my back on them.

It was a very small victory, a victory by omission rather than a genuine active resistance, but I was still very proud of myself.

***

Unlikely as it may sound, what follows is absolutely true.

I don't remember anything about the classical record, all I know is that it didn't interest me and I didn't spend much time with it.

I put *The King and I* on the turntable, hoping the music would be worthy of the album cover. The opening was pleasant enough in the Oriental-American style of the fifties, but it didn't really grab me and I nearly put the record back in its envelope. Then came the first song, "I Whistle a Happy Tune." The words leaped out at me like a message that Anna, the English school-mistress who had just arrived in Siam to teach the king's children, was sending out to me personally across time, a record, a film, a song and I was blown away:

"Whenever I feel afraid
I hold my head erect
And whistle a happy tune
So no one will suspect
I'm afraid."

The song was addressed to me personally! The secret was in its off-hand manner. If I wanted to get inside that theatre I had to be the opposite of the beaten dog who goes and hides in the corner so he'll be forgotten before he even gets scolded for doing something wrong! I had to be so offhand the cashier would feel she had to let me in even though she could see I wasn't sixteen yet. Most of all she mustn't know I was terrified of her. I shouldn't have run away, I should have faced up to her—holding my head erect.

***

I sped back to return the two records, telling the salesgirl in a superior tone: "They're boring!" and ran to the theatre without stopping.

The dragon was still at her post; there was no one going inside because the film had started ages ago. The cashier was listlessly leafing through a magazine while she waited for the next wave of customers who wouldn't turn up for an hour at least. I gathered up the small amount of courage I still had despite my wobbly legs, the sweat running down my back, my rapidly pounding heart and the lump in my throat and I managed to arrive at the ticket booth whistling, just like on the record. It wasn't very loud, but you could hear it. I don't know if you could really call it casual, but I hoped it would give the illusion. Bravely, I dropped my seventy-five cents in front of her, looking her straight in the eye. "Please God, don't let her recognize me! Don't let her create a scandal so I have to defend myself in English, I can't speak it well enough and I don't want to be laughed at on top of everything else!" Inwardly I was the Krakatoa about to erupt, but outwardly I wanted to give the impression I was someone for whom going to the movies was nothing out of the ordinary, a critic maybe, yes, why not, a rather blasé critic who's stuck with seeing this film he doesn't really want to see and he's going now, just before noon, so he won't ruin an entire day. Someone who couldn't care less if they let him in or not, because this film, really.... She probably didn't look at me or else she admired my nerve enough to disregard her rules and her convictions, but the fact remains that I ended up holding a ticket without having hell open up at my feet or lightning strike my slender little body. It was almost too easy, I hesitated for a fraction of a second before walking away from the cashier.

I had a ticket for *The King and I* two years early!

I'll always remember the state of euphoria I was in as I climbed the thickly-carpeted stairs. I looked at myself in the huge mirror that ran along the banister on both sides, multiplying my reflection infinitely.... Though I looked like a little bum! A little bum in his Sunday best who wants access to something he's unworthy of.... How could I deceive anybody? I was still whistling but my mouth was frozen, I felt as if never again would I be able to relax the muscles in my lips.

The ticket-taker didn't even look at me and I went down into the theatre deep in a Nirvana whose intensity measured 8.5 on the Richter scale.

It was a wall-to-wall screen, Cinemascope in all its splendor, and a Siamese ballet as revised by Rogers and Hammerstein was unfurling its extravagance while Rita Moreno intoned: "Run, little Eva, run!" I raced to the most anonymous seat, the one where nobody ever sits because it gives you a headache, and let myself be swallowed up for two and a half hours by the faintly sickening but oh so reassuring syrup of the colours, the music, the dances, the songs, the sets, the stunning dresses worn by Deborah Kerr (who would be the great idol of my teenage years, at least till the arrival of Shirley MacLaine

117

in *Some Came Running*), and the seductive outfits worn by Yul Brynner.

I was thrilled, moved, and I swore that from now on I was going to movies "for adults" at least once a week. No more silly kids' stuff for me; starting now, the global production of movies, at least whatever made it to Montreal, was mine. I was an adult.

Les Visiteurs du soir

A grouping of stone with a heart. A two-person grouping of stone with a single heart for the two. That beats. They embrace in a kiss for eternity and you can hear their heart beating through their stony bodies. Jules Berry, a brilliant demon, nearly likable in his malice because he's so charming, whips them, screaming: "It beats! It beats! It beats!" Marie Déa and Alain Cuny are frozen forever in the act of embracing. The love of an acrobat and a baroness has triumphed over all and now they are embracing in front of everyone for eternity. The end.

I'm sitting in my mother's rocking chair in front of the TV set. I haven't touched my pineapple upside-down cake, my glass of Quik still sits on the edge of the table, untouched. My father has come home from work and I barely said hello to him. Monsieur Migneault went to bed five minutes after it started, muttering: "Another goddamn ridiculous French show!" and I'm grateful to him. Soon it will be one a.m. Insulting our intelligence, "O Canada" oompahs while the Union Jack flaps. Someone tells us that broadcasting will resume tomorrow afternoon.

I'll never be the same again. A film shot during the war, under conditions and with a subtext I won't understand until much later has just transformed my life. The poetry of Prévert, the songs as much as the dialogues, have transported me into a world of whose existence I was totally unaware; Arletty's face turned my heart upside down, Alain Cuny's voice vibrated in me like a light. She, whom he calls his sister but who is his mistress, has discovered cynicism; he, love. With his script, his cast, his images, Marcel Carné has stirred up in my soul the emotions, the doubts, the questioning that will make me want to be a writer.

I write already, of course, my school compositions are praised, I concoct little things on my brother's typewriter, but till now I've been quite certain I was not worthy of the name writer or, rather, I was convinced I had no right to dream about writing as the official, the only acceptable, only viable way to express myself because I'd come from a background that doesn't produce artists unless they deny their roots and espouse the life and the ideas of a world supposedly superior and separate from theirs. I had no one to tell me if I was right or wrong, but that sense of unworthiness was deeply rooted in me.

And in an hour and a half it was all overturned for ever. I could never say how or why, maybe because of those poor troubadours who come to a castle and weaken its very foundations without really wanting to, through their mere presence, their mere existence; or perhaps it's because of their simplicity alongside the pretentiousness of the evil baron played by Fernand Ledoux, the affectedness of the demon, but I know that beginning tomorrow, in texts transposed if not poetic, I will try to say who I am, or at least try to do so through writing. I too can be hard-headed, I can believe despite the small chance I have of succeeding, I can persevere, dream if I have to, because you need a good dose of dreaming if you think you can produce publishable texts when you've turned your back on an official education, the great schools, college, university, to attempt, on your own, to build yourself a culture—imperfect, unruly, disparate, it's true—but at least personal. Like the lovers in the film, the poet and the married woman, who slip through everything because they believe they're right.

Starting now, I shall believe that it's legitimate for me to write.

The release mechanism I needed has shown itself and thanks to Monsieur Carné, to Monsieur Prévert, I'm going to be a writer no matter what the cost!

Still, I smile at my own naiveté as I get undressed. My sense of the ridiculous, somewhere between the pretentiousness of a talented adolescent and the terror of a child who's beginning to understand that the world is something other than a playground on a summer afternoon, that tendency I have not to take myself too seriously for too long sends me back a comical image of myself: the poor little bum from Cartier Street who wants to hoist himself up next to.... I don't even dare mention their names, just thinking about it seems ridiculous.

Better to take refuge in dreams, as usual, as I do after the Oscars when I can't get to sleep because I'm so envious of all those fancy people or after the crowning of Miss Radio-Cinema-Television because I'd like to be Denise Pelletier, actress of the year, or Marcel Dubé, who wrote the best play.... Before I fall asleep I dream of being part of that crowd, and I also dream about it after I'm asleep.

But another daydream is mixed in, is knitted to the first. Marie Déa and Alain Cuny, who refuse to yield, will be punished.... Only death can overcome their obstinacy. Jules Berry lifts his arm and the transformation, the punishment begin: Marie Déa's gown, Alain Cuny's legs turn to stone, their torsos too, and then before the stone steals over everything and blinds them for ever, they look at one another, embrace. And they're frozen in that position. But their heart, from now on just one heart for the two of them, continues to beat. They have not yielded.

They are victorious. And the baron (power?) and the demon (religion?) can't do anything about it.

***

The next day, after school, I start to write the little novel that follows. My first real steps.

New York, 17 April–24 July 1990

No Honour
Among Thieves

Michel Tremblay

translated by
Sheila Fischman

PUBLISHER'S NOTE

This short novel Michel Tremblay wrote at the age of 16 is presented here in its entirety, complete with all the naiveté and the audacity in its contents and the "imperfections" in its form.

Inside the big, overheated church were several hundred sweating people, squeezed four at a time into pews that only had room for three. From his pulpit the old priest was repeating for the sixth time that "Jesus came to earth to save us and we should thank him on this beautiful Christmas night." A few men, already drunk, were fast asleep, heads nestled in their winter coats. The women, faces painted and dressed to kill, appeared to be paying attention, but their minds were very far from the sermon by the priest, an old man who'd come down with the flu. The wide-eyed children were absorbing as much light as they could. They alone were thinking about the One who had just been born; they alone were watching the crèche in the hope of seeing the little bundle of frozen flesh start to move; they alone were waiting impatiently for the shepherds, the poor shepherds with their damp gifts.

"It is grace that I wish to you all, in the name of the Father and the Son and the Holy Ghost, amen."

All rose. Their heads still heavy with dreams, some of the sleepers wondered where they were. The coughers stopped coughing. The children reluctantly left the magical stable to join the grownups at the boring altar.

The Credo. "I believe in almighty God, the Father...." Eight hundred persons were reciting these words with only half a mind and the words they half forgot or omitted altogether removed any meaning from the prayer. The Credo. A long chain of words with a genuflection in the middle.

Everyone sat down again. The sleepers went back to sleep and the coughers went back to coughing. While up above, the choir was singing at the top of its lungs.

After a canon for three voices that made the old ladies weep and kept a few men from snoozing, came the elevation. Eight hundred prostrate bodies, eight hundred empty heads. The children had long since gone back to thinking about the crèche, the star, the angels who were singing hymns before hymns were even invented. A tinkling bell: isn't that a shepherd to announce the arrival of the Promised One? Another tinkling bell; all heads bow. Empty heads. Mechanically, some old ladies recite their morning prayer. A third bell; the same empty heads look up. The priest sneezed, isn't that funny! Just three more tinkling bells and they'll finally be able to get up....

When the organ starts to rumble again and the choir to bellow, half the audience turns around and looks up to see the cause of all this racket. They smile when Brother Isidore's organ sounds off-key in the very middle of a flight of pious notes.

Ite missa est. A little boy leans across to his mother: "Did you hear what the priest just said, Mummy? That's how *Maria Chapdelaine* starts! The very same words! I read the first page in my French book...."

The church has been half-empty for a while now.

"Aren't you staying for the three masses?"

"No. That's way too long."

The church steps are crawling with people. There are rich people with their golden smiles and poor people with no smiles at all; there are fat women dressed like fur-bearing animals and little women dressed like feather dusters; there are children wearing fur-lined boots and children in summer shoes.

"Merry Christmas!

"Merry Christmas, old man!"

Handshakes, hugs and kisses, kicks, elbows, saccharine smiles, hypocritical smiles, half-smiles, quarter-smiles, one-third smiles, and breaths that reeked of booze.

"Why don't you come over for réveillon?"

"I can't, dear, I'm invited to a friend's place...."

Taxis sit waiting across from the church. Automobile drivers fight over the road, an old lady who'd like to cross and doesn't dare for fear of being hit by one of these imbeciles stands on the corner, freezing.

The whole city is steeped in an atmosphere of false joy, joy manufactured from *tourtières* and alcoholic beverages. People have forgotten why they're celebrating. Forgotten whom they're celebrating. They decorate their houses with garlands, balls and icicles. And their souls? Sin is not a decoration! There's no snow. It hasn't really snowed yet this year but still it's very cold. A pale, icy cold runs across the deserted streets. Laughing, it rushes inside the houses of the poor and with sadistic pleasure slits their throats.

Christmas.

***

It was cold inside the taxi. On the back seat, Jocelyn was weeping. It had been so long since he'd cried! Months, maybe years, since he'd felt these cold little things running down his cheeks and the pain, just there, in his throat, the pain you feel when you're tired of crying. And Jocelyn was tired of crying. Already. When he'd started to feel the tears

129

flow, Jocelyn was happy. For a very brief moment he had savored this thing he'd rediscovered, that felt nearly new because it was forgotten. It was cold in the taxi. The tears froze on Jocelyn's cheeks and eyelashes. And Jocelyn was tired of crying.

When the car stopped in front of the house, a huge red brick dwelling with turrets and gables, with pointed roofs and windows as big as the stained-glass windows in a church—in short, one of those houses about which people say, the families that live there must be happy and united because they're rich. Jocelyn tried to wipe away one last tear, but the driver had seen. "Your love story didn't work out, eh, young fellow?"

Jocelyn shrugged and made no reply.

"Why exactly was I crying anyway? I don't know. It just came over me, like a craving for chocolate or ice cream...."

Big trees with frozen arms rushed past the car. In the inky sky the moon formed a brilliant stain, a white sin upon a black soul. She must be freezing for sure, perched up there so high!

"But there has to be a reason! You don't start to cry for no reason, just because you feel an urge."

The streets were deserted, bare, abandoned, but the windows were all lit up. In each of the houses of the rich, people were nibbling at a poor little piece of happiness for Christmas time. The trees rushed past the automobile faster and faster, as if they were afraid of missing an important date....

"I have to find out. I absolutely have to find out!"

***

"You haven't gone yet?"

Jocelyn had stopped in the middle of the vestibule and now was looking at his mother in her white gown (you know, the famous Dior gown, yes, that one, the dress she'd bought to wear at the Bal des petits souliers de satin rose, who was coming down the stairs, smoking a cigarette.

"Your father refuses to come to the réveillon with me. And of course he waited till I was dressed to let me know!"

An impatient gesture. "Where are the ashtrays...ah, yes..."

Christine Déjazet was very beautiful. There were even those who said she was the most beautiful woman in Montreal... But then, people say so many things.... She had a face that was fairly intelligent, which made up for the intelligence she did not possess, with deep green eyes (green as the sea, as certain poets, the bad ones, would say), a nose that was a little long but pretty anyway, a tiny mouth, turned up at the corners, which gave her a false resemblance to the Mona Lisa, or the look of a false Mona Lisa, and soft white cheeks punctuated by adorable little dimples. But what was most attractive about her was her forehead. It was magnificent. Intelligent. It immediately drew your attention. It possessed that certain something that makes us say a forehead is intelligent. Was it its breadth? Its whiteness? No. Yes, maybe. The fact was, she was unaware that she had a beautiful forehead. And so she didn't hide it. On the contrary. She had always worn her hair in such a way as to show off her forehead. She looked very intelligent—as long as her forehead was uncovered. If it was hidden, her face was still very beautiful but it lost its personality and intelligence. Christine carried her thirty-nine years wonderfully well. She looked maybe thirty, no more. Madame Lebrun, a jealous soul, said that she was well-preserved. Ought to be mummified. "She must have discovered the secret of the Egyptians."

Seeing her standing there in the vestibule in all her splendor, Jocelyn thought back to what Monsieur Coutu had told him a few days earlier: "Young man, you're lucky to have such a beautiful young mother. Make sure you hold on to her for a long time." How could a person make such an idiotic remark! Yes, she's beautiful, agreed, but she's not all that young. As for holding on to her for a long time…. I'd rather trade her in on an ugly old mother, a real one. The woman's not a real mother.

That, Jocelyn had known for a long time. While still very young he had realized that his mother was not one, that she didn't know how to bring him up the way a boy should be brought up, that she loved him not as you love a boy, but as you love a doll. He had always been Christine's darling doll, her wonderful toy.

One, two, three, four large diamonds paraded across her scarcely veiled bosom. "Mama only has horrible jewels…."

For some moments now Christine had worn a strange expression. She came up to her son and ran her fingernail across one of his cheeks.

"You've been crying. Why have you been crying?"

"I wasn't crying, Christine. It's because it was cold."

"Oh yes you were! I know you were. I can sense it. My poor darling, are you sad? Why are you sad?"

"Leave me alone! If I've been crying it's my business, isn't it? Quit bothering me!"

One can become accustomed to anything. Even to that? Christine asked herself. "That's something I could never get used to…. One simply does not speak to one's mother like that…."

Christine Déjazet walked into the living room just as Jocelyn was starting up the stairs. She stretched out rather than sat in the big black and gold armchair at the back of the room. Where it was darkest. At the very back of the living room. Why so far away? Why at the back of the room precisely? She took her head in her hands.

"I'll never get used to it. Though I was the one who wanted it that way. I should never have allowed it when he first started speaking to me like that at such a young age. I thought it was funny. I enjoyed it when he lost his temper. But he's too old for that now. Now what he says is wounding. How hard it is to bring up children! Good thing I don't have more."

Raising her head, she realized where she was. "Now that's strange. I always sit here when I'm sad. In this black armchair. I wonder why...."

She got up, headed for the bar. She took down a bottle at random. "What a peculiar colour!" The drink was a rather repulsive yellowish green. Christine repeated, "What a peculiar colour." She used the word "peculiar" almost constantly. For her everything was peculiar. "What a peculiar colour, what a peculiar hat, look, isn't that peculiar, a peculiar man...." She was not aware of it, but for those around her it eventually grew irritating. She made a face as she swallowed the drink she'd poured. How nasty it can be! She shuddered. Another. Jocelyn has gone up to his room. Oh, I nearly forgot!

"Jocelyn! Jocelyn, can you hear me?"

"What do you want?"

"What are you doing?"

"Getting undressed. I can do it all by myself now, you know!"

"Don't get undressed. You'll come to the Coutus' with me."

A brief silence. A door opens. Footsteps. Then Jocelyn appears at the top of the stairs.

He doesn't look as if he's in complete agreement. Oh! the drink is starting to have an effect!

"Christine, you know perfectly well how I hate parties!"

"Just as a favour to me, pet! Please! Can you see me turning up at the Coutus' by myself? What would people say? Whereas if you're with me...."

"What did you and Papa fight about?"

"Papa? You call him 'Papa' now? What's come over you? You're not so respectful with me!"

"Please, answer my question. Why?"

"As you know all too well, your father and I always argue over the slightest thing. I can't even remember why he doesn't want to come...but you will, won't you? When it's just to make me happy? I absolutely insist on going to the Coutus' réveillon. You know how beautifully they entertain...."

Jocelyn had gone back to his room without responding.

Christine took off one of her bracelets, which was pinching her wrist. Rubbing the little red mark left by the gold, she made her way towards the armchair at the back of the living room. "So much for my evening," she thought, closing her eyes. "I don't even know if I'm sorry." She was not yet disappointed. Yet she'd been delighted to accept Angéline's invitation. "By chance, we had no plans for Christmas Eve this year. As my parents had died recently and Georges's were in Europe...." She had received a card from Paris. A postcard. Not a letter. Very small, the card. And signed: M. et Mme Déjazet. There was also a brief message: "Paris is beautiful but we miss the snow. Having a wonderful time." "Yet they ought to know there's been no snow here either. When they left two weeks ago it was nearly warm."

No, she was not disappointed, not yet. She felt only an emptiness inside her as when you've burned your foot but haven't yet had time to feel the pain. But perhaps it was also the effect of the drink. "It doesn't take much."

She recalled the day, the famous day when she'd got drunk in her parents' basement because they'd refused to let her go out. "I took a bottle of red wine and I drank it all down there. And oh my, how sick I was afterwards."

Without thinking, without even wanting to, she got up as if moved by a hairspring and poured herself another drink. She saw her father again. Henri Monnet. The same Henri Monnet who twenty years earlier had written a five-volume work on *The Private Life of the Bee.* "I was so fond of Papa. A kind man. A darling." Then she thought about his body, about his dead body that even now was freezing somewhere, over in the Côte-des-Neiges cemetery; about his body that must be half-decomposed now, that must be a hideous sight to see. "But no one will ever see it again. No one can ever be afraid of my father's body.... How can it be that I'm holding a glass? And it's half-empty again! No, no one will be able...only at the end of the world. Then I'll see Papa again. But will I recognize him? How old will he be after the Last Judgment? The age he was when he died? Then I pity Methuselah!"

Christine started to laugh. "Methuselah. What a name! The Bible is full of outlandish names like that. Nebuchadnezzar." She started to spell the name of N-E-B-U-C-H-A-D-N-E-Z-Z-A-R. "I can't remember if it has an H or not." Then all at once she felt let down. Suddenly sad. But it was a vague sadness, like a shadow;

135

no, like a shadow passing in the shadows, that one tries to identify. "I can't remember why I'm disappointed. But it doesn't matter, I still feel like crying. In fact I think I'm crying already. Like Jocelyn. Jocelyn cried on his way home from midnight mass. Oh! I just remembered why I'm sad." That was enough to make her sadness end. "It's not that important. I'll go to the Coutus' another time." Still, what a brute he was, Georges! To spoil her pleasure like that. She thought she was falling asleep but realized that on the contrary, she was waking up.

A very handsome young man was standing before her. He hadn't yet had time to take his hand from Christine's shoulder.

"Oh, it's you, Jocelyn. I hadn't realized you were so handsome."

"And yet," thought Jocelyn, "you haven't stopped looking at me since I was born."

"I've decided to go to that réveillon with you, Christine. It will be your Christmas present. But we'll have to get moving, it's already late."

"Was I asleep very long?"

"A quarter of an hour at most. It's two o'clock."

"In the morning?"

∗∗∗

"Don't drive so fast, Jocelyn, you'll get us killed! This is no time to have an accident! What would your father say if he could see you driving his car as if it were a vulgar bicycle?"

His mother's voice, like a crow's, always brought him back to reality a little too brutally. Already when he was little he dared not dream in his mother's presence, because he knew that her loathsome voice would ruin his dream and then he'd be annoyed with her for waking him abruptly.

All at once Jocelyn slammed on the brakes. Crying out, Christine nearly went through the windshield.

"Are you out of your mind? What's come over you?"

Jocelyn knew. He knew why he'd been crying in the taxi; he knew why he'd wanted to go to bed when he got home and why he didn't feel like going to the Coutus' réveillon; he knew why he'd thought about that horrible thing—death—in his bath the other day. Sylvain! It was because of Sylvain!

Jocelyn sought a quiet spot where he could think.

He had cried because of Sylvain! When Sylvain told him he was going away forever he'd been sad, but from there to bursting into tears....

The house was packed with people and there wasn't a single place that wasn't occupied by one of Madame's friends or relatives. Jocelyn finally settled into an ugly little sofa by the fireplace, between a long dried-out woman with waxy skin and a tall anemic individual with green hands who was talking to himself.

Even after Sylvain had gone, he hadn't cried. But now, this evening, nearly two months later.... "I don't get it. And yet I'm sure I cried because of him!"

A huge fire was blazing in the fireplace, sending out golden sparks and creating the shadows of furious ghosts. It reminded Jocelyn of a certain evening when he'd stayed over at Sylvain's; a certain evening when, lying in front of the fireplace with his friend, it had seemed to him for the first time that.... "No, that's impossible. I'm normal. Even if I'm not attracted to girls, it doesn't mean I'm.... But if girls don't attract me, it's because there's something wrong...."

The wax woman leaned over to Jocelyn: "Excuse me, young man, but are you the son of Monsieur and Madame Déjazet?" The woman's name was Joséphine Prud'homme. "You know, the florist, yes, that's right, the florist at Larose. You didn't recognize me, did you? It's been so long.... Not many deaths in your family this past while. Mind you, I'm very happy for you. But perhaps you've changed florists? What a lovely ring you're wearing." "Oh, shut your trap!" Jocelyn felt like exclaiming, but he excused himself politely and took his leave of her. "I won't be able to think things over comfortably tonight. I'll have to wait. Again."

Angéline Coutu leaned over the shoulder of Madame Du Tremblay, a phony noblewoman who had added a "Du" to her name which was far too common for a wealthy person, and said: "Look, Christine Déjazet's just arrived. Watch how she struts about. She's a little too aware that she's beautiful for her age!"

"Beautiful, her?" exclaimed Madame Du Tremblay. "You mean her mask is beautiful! She's wearing more makeup than a circus clown! And as for her age, you know...."

The two women laughed very softly (they mustn't be overheard by someone who would then ask why they were laughing, what could they—friends of Madame Déjazet—have replied?)

Angéline had always loathed Christine Déjazet, but she didn't let it show, especially not in front of Madame Déjazet herself, so that the other woman considered her to be her closest friend. Angéline envied Christine her beauty. Ugly as sin herself, she could not bear it that a woman lower than she on the social ladder should be superior to her in beauty. As for Madame Du Tremblay, she envied Madame Déjazet her youth; she even tried to convince people that Christine was much older than she let on.

"Watch out, she's coming this way," Angéline whispered. When Christine saw that her friend was with Madame Du Tremblay, she scowled. The Du Tremblay woman got on her nerves with her fake noble behaviour. "The old Jezebel! One of these days I'm going to tell her...." Smiling, she held out her hand to Robertine Du Tremblay. "How are you, dear friend?" She had bitten into the "dear friend" as one bites into a lemon; Robertine Du Tremblay swallowed it as one swallows castor oil.

"You're rather late, darling," murmured Angéline. "Where's your husband?"

"He had a dreadful headache, of all things. But I've brought Jocelyn with me." Jocelyn shook the hand Angéline held out and bowed slightly to Madame Du Tremblay.

"I'm so glad you're here," said Angéline Coutu. "As it happens I have a beautiful young lady I'd like you to meet."

"Oh yes?" Jocelyn pretended to be pleased. " Then I'd love to meet her."

Christine was virtually lying down between Angéline and Madame Du Tremblay. Jocelyn looked away to avoid seeing her.

Everything in this house that was far too big for two people oozed wealth and bad taste. Jocelyn thought the Coutus had decorated their house without a shred, without even a hint of good taste. Quite unscrupulously they had combined the ancient and the modern, which gave the rooms a style that made no sense at all. Other people though it very original and never failed to congratulate the Coutus on their ingenuity, but in Jocelyn's opinion it was hideous. The living room was somewhere between two greens that made him sick to his stomach. The furniture, pink and red, was in Louis XV style, while the walls were hung with modern paintings, which on top of everything else were ugly as sin. The woollen carpet was the same green as the walls. "If I were them I'd be ashamed to have a living room like this," thought Jocelyn.

Madame Coutu was very proud of her house, particularly the living room. "It's taken my husband and me years," she said to anyone who would listen, "to put our house together, and I think we're entitled to be proud of what we've done. People envy us our red-and-green living room. Everywhere people are copying us!"

When Jocelyn walked into this house he felt uneasy. He couldn't have explained why, but the house made him want to vomit.

Jocelyn sat in a big red armchair and closed his eyes. He would have liked to reflect for a moment, one very brief moment, but just try thinking in the midst of a hullabaloo like this! People were shouting, dancing, laughing: the idiots. On the orange sofa, Christine and her two friends were laughing very loud. "They must be tearing someone to shreds," thought Jocelyn.

∗∗∗

A stooped little old lady walked past him. "Good evening, young man," she chirped in a voice like a cricket's, "How are you? I've just noticed your mother, she gets younger every day...." Jocelyn hadn't had time to open his mouth when already the old lady had melted into a group of little old people disguised as young.

∗∗∗

"Your son is very pensive, Christine, is anything wrong?"

"I don't know what it is, he's been acting strangely for a while now. When he came back from midnight mass I realized he'd been crying. But he wouldn't tell me a thing. He even denied he'd been crying."

"Young people are very emotional, you know. And besides, your son has just lost a friend...."

"Surely that's not why he was crying.... Anyway, Sylvain has been gone for two months."

"Perhaps he was more attached to that Sylvain than you think...."

***

She came back to sit with her son.

"You're not yourself this evening, Jocelyn. Is something wrong?"

"I should have listened to myself and not come to this réveillon! All these pretentious people get on my nerves! Look at our hostess, carrying on like a trained monkey! The way she's dressed, you wonder if she's a woman or a bundle of rags!"

***

Madame Déjazet burst out laughing. "You're wonderful when you're angry, Jocelyn! I adore you!" She leaned across to her son and applied her lips to his forehead. Jocelyn thought he would die of shame.

***

141

Angéline Coutu came a little closer to Madame Du Tremblay. "I'm sure you're aware, my dear, that Madame Déjazet's son is a pederast."

∗∗∗

From the moment she first noticed Jocelyn, Isabelle was struck by his beauty. Such a beautiful boy. Maybe even too beautiful for a boy. The exceptional sweetness in his gaze pleased the young girl right away. Jocelyn looked a lot like the young woman with whom he was talking; was she his sister? But then perhaps it was his mother, after all not everyone has parents as old as mine. I don't know who they are. Friends of my aunt, most likely....

∗∗∗

"Did you see the look on his face when I told him I wanted to introduce him to a girl? He did his best to look normal, but you can't fool Angéline Coutu. There's no doubt about it, he is one! In fact, you know what they were saying about his friendship with the young son of the new Canadian ambassador to.... But I'm going to introduce him to Isabelle now, my sister Georgette's daughter. She's a delightful young girl and I'll say no more—but we'll see how he reacts."

∗∗∗

A few seconds later, Isabelle and Jocelyn had been introduced. "He's even more handsome up close," thought Isabelle. "She's not ugly, she's actually rather pretty," thought Jocelyn. Neither was speaking. Isabelle was looking at the boy's eyes. Amazing eyes! And so big! Green, slightly brownish. Isabelle felt all warm inside. "Could this be what it's like, to fall in love at first sight?"

Finally Jocelyn decided to say something.

"Are you still at school?"

"Yes, high school." Jocelyn liked her voice. "What about you?"

"I'm at classical college. In rhetoric."

She enjoyed reading and movies, he liked the theatre and music. Especially opera.

"Opera? I hate opera. I can't bear those long calculated, numbered shouts. Besides, opera libretti are all ridiculous."

"Opera libretti are *not* all ridiculous! And if the libretto is absurd, the music makes up for it. Take *Il Trovatore*, for instance, it's true the story is totally idiotic, but the music...."

They parted rather coolly. A difference of opinion. Isabelle refused to admit that Gangrène's books were just as idiotic as some opera libretti—if not more so. She had read almost everything by Gangrène. Who was her favorite author. And her favourite actor was Georges Sandrin. Georges Sandrin! Jocelyn couldn't get over it.

"All he can do is cloak-and-dagger films."

"He's very handsome and...."

"So that's it! He's handsome! I beg you, don't confuse beauty and talent! And as for talent, he has none."

"You're just jealous!"

Isabelle immediately regretted her remark. How could Jocelyn be jealous of Georges Sandrin's looks when he was so much more handsome? Isabelle apologized.

Jocelyn was offended. Him, jealous? They parted rather coolly. "I think my mother wants me...."

***

"What did you think of her?" asked Christine.

"A featherbrain! Gangrène and Georges Sandrin!"

Jocelyn put an end to the conversation with a wave of his hand that seemed to sweep from his mind Isabelle, Gangrène, Georges Sandrin, and many other things as well....

***

"What do you think of him?"

"Not bad, but his tastes are odd!"

"Watch out for him, dear, he can't really be recommended...."

"Then why did you introduce us?"

"Come, I'll explain everything...."

***

"Madame is served."

Then came the rush. Like a flock of vultures swooping down on a fresh corpse. Outstretched arms, laughter, pushing, envious looks, plunging hands, laughter....

At the other end of the table sat a young boy of about sixteen who was picking at a pink sandwich. Jocelyn noticed him right away. "How sad he looks! I wonder who he is." The young boy looked up and saw Jocelyn. The two gazed at one another for a few moments, neither one able to look away. Jocelyn smiled.

"What did I tell you? See how he's looking at young Éric Koestler, as if he wanted to eat him up!"

Éric looked away first. He put down his sandwich and didn't eat anything more.

***

"He's Éric Koestler. His parents are new friends of Madame Coutu's. Would you like to be introduced?"

"No, no, I just wondered what his name was."

He didn't want to be introduced to him right away. He feared that first meeting. He sensed the need to befriend this fair-haired boy, but he was afraid their first meeting would be a fiasco like his meeting with Isabelle. "Isabelle's a girl, it's not the same," he thought, to reassure himself. "I don't have a knack for making friends with girls. I'm awkward with them and they laugh at me."

Éric, who was sitting at the other end of the living room, appeared to be bored to death. Every three or four minutes he covered his face politely and yawned.

Angéline Coutu entered the living room, followed by her pretty niece in a chiffon gown, who pretended not to notice Jocelyn who was looking at her severely. The two women made their way to Éric. Angéline introduced Isabelle to him. Jocelyn got up, furious. He couldn't have said why, but he was suddenly filled with a horrible anger. He crossed the room, nearly running, and planted himself in front of Éric. Angéline had no choice but to introduce Éric to Jocelyn, which she did grudgingly as a matter of fact. Smiling awkwardly, Jocelyn tried to say something pleasant but the sounds absolutely refused to come out of his mouth. He could only proffer a sort of hoarse groan that made Isabelle laugh. Red as a peony, he made a ridiculous little bow to Éric and went back to his seat.

***

"Did you see what he's wearing? I've never seen a boy dressed like that! He could compete with any movie star, easily. A man mustn't dress too well. That should be left to women. Take my husband for instance, it's been at least three years since he bought himself a suit! He's not well dressed and I wouldn't want him to be. Leave the fine clothes to effeminate boys like Jocelyn. God, how I could hate him! Only yesterday I ran into him on Sherbrooke Street. You should have seen him! He was wearing a very pale, very short overcoat, suede, with a narrow belt at the waist; very tight black pants (you know, the kind a ballet dancer might wear) and Russian boots. I wanted to scratch him. I pretended not to see him and I didn't say hello."

∗∗∗

That made three times his mother had pinched him. "Smile, smile!" He'd smiled quite enough! "We don't have to smile just because we're at a réveillon! Besides, I don't even like réveillons! I don't feel like smiling and I'm not going to. Let her pinch me all she wants, it won't make any difference!" Madame Koestler insisted that her son smile. A well brought-up boy must be able to smile even if he doesn't feel like it; a well brought-up boy must never let others guess his feelings when they're not appropriate, a well brought-up boy…. "You always have such a long face! People will think you're sick! I'm warning you, if you have that ridiculous look tonight at the réveillon I'll punish you tomorrow morning, even though it's Christmas!" "Even though I'm too old for her punishments. And if she does punish me, I'll just hate her a little more, that's all!"

Éric took a small sandwich from the large silver salver. Who had the bright idea of making pink sandwiches! And green ones! And yellow! Looking up, Éric spied Jocelyn looking at him from the other end of the table.

Immediately, the sad young boy struck him as likable. And when the unknown boy smiled at him, he felt something warm, something new rising in him. It fluttered through his stomach and he shivered. Now it was going to his head as if he'd been drinking champagne. And his hunger, the intolerable hunger that had tormented him all evening, flew away. Was this the friend he had so long been waiting for? Was it finally him, the one with whom he could talk freely about his joys and sorrows without fear of rebuke or laughter? Was this finally the friend, the genuine one? Trembling, he set down his sandwich.

***

Everything in the living room seemed to be spinning. The walls, the floor, the furniture doubled, rose and fell as they spun around Jocelyn. Closing his eyes, he held his head in his hands. A needle, long and sharp, pierced his skull at regular intervals. Nearly imperceptible at first, the pain intensified until it became unbearable, then it slowly departed, only to come back more severe than ever. Jocelyn wanted to cry out but he restrained himself so as not to attract attention, so that no one would realize he was suffering, ashamed as never before in his life. He'd made a fool of himself like a vulgar imbecile! He wanted to die. He heard Isabelle's crystalline laughter and wished he could jump on her and rip that laughter from her throat like a rotten tooth. Then slowly he calmed down. The pain had gone, Jocelyn opened his eyes. The furniture had stopped dancing and Éric was sitting on the sofa beside him.

***

A tango. A crazed woman and a naval officer began to fly about the living room. The woman seemed to be drowning in happiness in the officer's arms, while the man was peering deep into the low-cut dress that gave him a glimpse of the buoys he lusted after. With lengthy strides, the couple sailed across the hardwood floor. The woman let out a long sigh. "The sea," she whispered, "what a beautiful thing it is, don't you agree? You, Monsieur, remind me of the sea, of crossings on the great ocean liners. I love the sea so much it makes me swoon! And I have my sea legs, you know! I've never been sick on board a ship. This tango is divine!" She rested her goose's head on the broad hairy chest (it must be hairy, all sailors have hairy chests) of the officer.

"I've got her!" he thought to himself. And in a gentle voice that surprised even him, he whispered in his dancing partner's ear: "You are my ideal of a woman, Madame. I like women who are small and plump like you, they have both character and masses of charm. It's a lucky thing for me that I must leave the day after tomorrow, for I think if I were to stay a little longer I would be ensnared by love. For the first time in my life!" The woman, half-dead, made no reply. The tango ended. "What a pity," murmured the officer, "we were so good together!" Bowing gracefully to his dancing partner he said: "I hope from the bottom of my heart that you'll save the next tango for me."

"Whatever you want, Monsieur," replied the woman, "whatever you want!"

"You shameless old charmer!" thought the officer as he moved away from the woman who was fanning herself to keep from fainting.

★★★

"Ridiculous, aren't they?" said Éric, pointing to the woman and the old sailor.

"Absolutely ridiculous," Jocelyn managed to get out, overcoming his embarrassment.

"Don't you feel well?" asked Éric. "You had a dizzy spell just now...."

"It's nothing," replied Jocelyn briskly. "I'm probably just tired."

"I don't know why, but Madame Coutu looked furious when she left the living room with her niece...."

Jocelyn lowered his gaze. After all, he couldn't admit that he was jealous! Jealous? But of what? Of whom? He had no reason to be jealous! All at once, he had a horrible thought. "No! It's impossible! It makes no sense! I didn't want Isabelle to meet Éric, I admit, but was it because of Isabelle—or Éric? Good God! And if.... No! I don't want that! It has to be because of Isabelle! It has to be because of Isabelle!"

For some moments now Éric had been observing the other boy. He liked the face but what was there behind the face? What was going on behind that forehead damp with sweat? Why was Jocelyn not looking at him directly? Éric got up to leave but Jocelyn made a move to stop him.

"You were looking pensive," said Éric, "I thought you wanted to be alone."

"No, I'd prefer it if you stay. It's so tiresome here! I'm bored in the company of those idiots...."

For the rest of the evening, Jocelyn and Éric chatted. Jocelyn felt springing up in him a desire to banish Éric from his life forever, to offend him so he'd go away, but wasn't it he who had asked Éric to stay just now? "After all, Éric will be an excellent friend. And those ideas that have been running through my head for a while now are absurd. It's impossible that I'm like that! It's impossible that I've fallen so low! Just now I was afraid Éric and Isabelle were getting interested in each other. I think I'm quite fond of Isabelle, in spite of her strange ideas. That's the reason for my machinations. I mustn't look any farther." But Jocelyn was less reassured than he wanted to believe....

✳✳✳

There are times when a person makes some remark that doesn't immediately strike us; but when we think about it again later, that remark, often very banal, takes on an exaggerated significance in our minds. It appears first of all in the form of some memory or other, then it attracts our attention. We study it for a few moments without knowing why it's attracting our attention; it becomes clearer, expands, even becomes obsessive. That scrap of a sentence whose meaning we hadn't immediately grasped is imprinted so indelibly on our memories, we can't get rid of it. We wonder what exactly the person in question was trying to say. Then a few days later the thing becomes so enormous, it finally bursts. But then the obvious truth (sometimes not obvious at all but we think it is) appears to us. And we panic, get worked up, get angry. Now nothing else matters to us: the thing haunts us and for a while it takes up most of the room in our lives. Giving too much meaning to something trivial, we almost call it a scandal. We designate as slander something that most of the time is nothing but chitchat. We think about all the people who have heard the remark and we feel like martyrs. We imagine that everybody knows such-and-such a thing and then, slowly, we calm down again. The thing assumes less importance and in the end we even forget it. And should it happen that we do think about it again, we call ourselves an idiot, a triple nitwit. We were imagining things that weren't true, we thought everybody knew certain things that only we were aware of....

Madame Déjazet was dozing. Resting uncomfortably against the door of the car as it fled across the wet streets of the sleeping city, she went over the whole evening when, all in all, she had been bored to death. She hadn't enjoyed herself as she had last year or the year before, the time, the famous time when Madame Thiboutot created a scene with her husband because he'd danced a little too often with...with.... "What's her name? She's on television in that...what's the name of the show she's on.... My ideas are definitely all tangled up! We were right to leave when we did!"

Jocelyn saw his mother raise her arm and open her mouth as if she wanted to speak, but then she seemed to change her mind because a moment later she dropped her arm and closed her mouth. "Did you have a good time at the party, Mama?" he asked, for something to say. His mother did not respond right away. Perhaps she was trying to put together a decent reply, but Jocelyn doubted she was capable of constructing one in the state she was in.... "No," was her simple reply a moment later. "Usually you enjoy the Coutus' parties, Mama. You always say they entertain so beautifully...." Christine said nothing. Jocelyn thought she'd fallen asleep. But no, Christine wasn't sleeping. On the contrary. Something, some remark Angéline had made about her son, had just come back to her and had her completely awake: some remark of which she was seeking the meaning, in vain. When Angéline had said: "Maybe he was more attached to that Sylvain than you think," Christine had paid no attention, but now that remark was running through the head of Jocelyn's mother. "Sylvain and Jocelyn were or rather they had been good friends, excellent comrades, and they were fond of one another, but why that remark by Madame Coutu? Why that 'more than you think'? Jocelyn certainly wasn't...." Christine started, violently. Jocelyn thought she was dreaming and nudged her to wake her up. "Was that what Angéline was trying to insinuate? No, that's unlikely, impossible even, my best friend...and yet...." And then bits of sentences she'd been overhearing here and there in the past year came back to her. When Sylvain and her son went out together evenings, people looked at them strangely and whispered as they passed. Christine had observed it several times last winter. And this summer, at Laval-sur-le-Lac, they were never invited to parties; Christine had thought it was because people knew that Jocelyn and Sylvain didn't like to dance and preferred classical music to the popular music, which Sylvain in fact referred to as "primitive." How blind she had been! It was because they were thought to be abnormal that they were kept out of a number of places! Christine had never thought about it. Did Jocelyn even suspect it? Surely not! The poor boy, how sad he would be if he knew the truth! The truth! But maybe not, it would be too horrible if people were right.... Jocelyn, her child, couldn't be like that!

For days Madame Déjazet could think about nothing else: was her son a homosexual or wasn't he? Oh, how that word turned her stomach! Come now, Jocelyn couldn't be one of those monsters, one of those wretches of society, it was unthinkable! She no longer slept, no longer ate, no longer spoke even, which was a sign that she was terribly preoccupied. Jocelyn had seen his mother in this state just once before, a few years ago when Christine had thought she was pregnant: for days she had cried continually and hadn't eaten and hadn't slept and hadn't spoken, but everything had returned to normal when the doctor told her she was mistaken, that she wasn't expecting a baby. Then it was as if there was a party in the house. All at once Christine had started talking again. And eating enough for four. That was when Jocelyn had started to hate his mother. He had taken it into his head, perhaps wrongly, that he had been an accident in his parents' lives, that they hadn't wanted him and that he'd been completely unwelcome. His mother had become a sort of monster in his eyes, a beautiful, well-dressed monster, but one whose voice gave her away. But was it just a voice? When Christine opened her mouth to speak, Jocelyn grew tense. He had dreamed for long nights that his mother was mute. She tried to talk, but in vain. All that came from her mouth was toads. And Jocelyn laughed and laughed…. He woke up dripping sweat and with tears in his eyes. And the terrible reality swooped down on him: his mother was speaking. Had it not been for that voice, Jocelyn would have forgiven his mother for many things, even perhaps for everything. But there was that voice of hers, that sort of hoarse croak that seemed to come directly from hell, that cawing voice that made him shudder. His mother's talking made Jocelyn's stomach ache.

He had noticed her looking at him strangely since the réveillon, but he didn't pay too much attention. She wasn't speaking to him, he couldn't ask for anything more. The Christmas holidays were quietly crumbling away, grey and dull. Every afternoon Jocelyn read and listened to records. After supper, he went out alone. He would walk for hours in this city that was more and more hostile to him, this hideous city with its broken streets where he felt so alone. If only Sylvain had been there! When he thought about Sylvain, Jocelyn turned even gloomier. He saw his friend again on the evening of his departure, carrying over his arm the raincoat he liked so much. He saw again the airport all lit up, the damned airport that had dealt the death blow to their friendship. He saw again Sylvain's tear-streaked face and he heard…. Oh! would it always be there in every one of his memories, his mother's voice bidding her son's friend farewell? Even that moment Christine had spoiled! When he came down for breakfast the next morning, Jocelyn saw his mother sitting over a cold cup of coffee. When he came in, she forced herself to take a sip, making a face as she swallowed. Neither of them said anything; Christine stared into the bottom of her cup and Jocelyn quietly buttered the toast that he wouldn't eat. Christine seemed to want to say something to her son: now and then she opened her mouth or moved slightly as if she wanted to speak, but she changed her mind every time and remained silent. Jocelyn could have sworn that his mother had something serious to say or to discuss with him but was too shy to do so. "Surely she doesn't want to tell me the facts of life?" he mused one day, smiling. "It's a little late for that. I waited so long until I gave up and had to find out elsewhere! If that's what she wants to talk to me about, I can understand why she's uncomfortable! It's not at the age of eighteen that a boy should learn...things. He starts wondering about them long before that, which is something parents cannot or will not understand. Deep down, I'm glad Mama didn't tell me anything; coming from her those things would have been ugly, while coming from...but who was it who actually told me? Oh! Yes! I remember: it was Sylvain's mother. I learned about everything at the same time he did. How shy we were and how we blushed when we asked her to explain...all those wonderful things...."

"Jocelyn...."

For the first time in days, his mother had spoken. Startled, Jocelyn looked at her over his steaming cup.

"So," he said indifferently, "you haven't lost your voice after all. I thought...."

"I have to talk to you, Jocelyn. Seriously."

"That's it," thought Jocelyn, "here it comes! *That!*"

"It's a delicate matter," his mother went on. "A matter that's very hard to bring up without insulting someone. But I beg you, after you've heard me out don't be angry, don't be shocked. I need to know, a mother needs to know everything about her son, you understand."

154

Jocelyn said nothing. Christine was more and more ill at ease. She stammered pitifully, wringing her hands. Jocelyn thought about actresses who think that any woman who's suffering has to wring her hands. Then he began to picture his mother as "la dame aux camélias." The only thing missing was the cough. Jocelyn started to cough.

"Have you caught cold?"

"No."

"You have to listen to me to the end, without interrupting and, I repeat, without getting angry. I know you're a man now, and that you may have your own ideas about certain things, but you're still very young and someone can have a bad influence on you...."

"What do you mean?" Jocelyn exclaimed.

"I told you not to interrupt," Christine snapped. "I don't know all your friends and some of them may not be very honorable. If that's the case, and only if that's the case, I might be able to understand your behaviour."

Christine was speaking faster and faster and her voice was becoming unbearable to Jocelyn. "I wish she'd shut up, if she doesn't shut up I'll go stark raving mad!" Jocelyn could no longer understand what his mother was saying, it was nothing but a flood, a tidal wave of words that surged into his mind and swept everything away. Christine's voice was now at fever pitch and Jocelyn began to tremble. His mother had not looked at him for some time. "What she's telling me must be serious," he thought, "but I can't grasp her words.... I can't!"

But now one word that had come from Christine's mouth whistled across the room, bouncing from wall to wall, gliding over the rug and onto the furniture, passing through mirrors and echoing endlessly; a word that was a slap in Jocelyn's face. Homosexual. The word took hold of him completely, shaking him, paralyzing him. Jocelyn thought his mother should have died for uttering that cursed word, for having dared to utter that word he had been struggling against for days and days. The walls parted like a theatre curtain and Jocelyn saw himself on a big stage, naked and alone, eyes glued to a multitude of individuals who were laughing their heads off at the sight of him there in the huge hall, intimidated. Then the crowd stopped laughing. Some men got to their feet, fists in the air, shouting: "Homosexual! Homosexual!" Though he plugged his ears, Jocelyn could hear them all the same. He wanted to leave this stage, this hall whatever the cost, but his feet were nailed to the boards and he couldn't move. All at once the curtain began to shudder but did not actually fall. And the hall continued to shout: "Homosexual! Homo…." When he opened his eyes again, at first Jocelyn saw only a piece of the ceiling from the middle of which hung a pale green chandelier. Then his mother's voice, grating on his ears: "Jocelyn, what's wrong? Dear God, he's fainted! Henri, Henri, bring me some cold water, Monsieur Jocelyn is feeling faint!" She bent over him and saw that he was crying. "I'm sorry," she said, "I'm sorry, Jocelyn. I didn't know I would hurt you so much! I just wanted to know! Ever since Christmas I've been brooding over that horrible thing in silence, so you'll understand that I had to know! I had to know! Jocelyn, answer me! I trust you and I'm certain you're not a homosexual." Jocelyn leaped up and slapped his mother full on the face. "You dared to think that of me! I hate you, I hate you, I'll always hate you! You're nothing but a, a…." He could not go on, the word was caught in his throat and he thought it was going to explode. His only sound was a loud cry, then he swept out, knocking over Henri and his water. He went up to his room and threw himself onto his unmade bed, thinking he was going to kill himself.

Right away, at once, you mustn't wait! Later on you won't be brave enough! Get up and do it! A razor blade, I need a razor blade, where can I find one? Apparently it doesn't hurt, you don't feel anything if you keep your hand in warm water. Be brave, Jocelyn, in a few minutes it will all be over, you won't be unhappy any more. They'll find you in the bathtub, in the bathtub filled with your blood. Don't tremble, it won't be that terrible! Just a little cut, it doesn't hurt! And you'll keep your hand in the water! A razor blade, I need a razor blade.... Imbeciles! They're imbeciles! To think that of me! But I'm normal! Absolutely normal! But then, maybe I'm not! No! I'm normal! I'll show them what I can do! When they find my body they'll have to face facts! Facts? What facts? Maybe when they find me they'll think my act was a confession that.... Apparently all homosexuals turn to suicide at some point.... I'm not even free to kill myself!

Montreal, 1959.